MEXICAN POPULAR ARTS

By Frances Toor

Illustrated by L. Alice Wilson

Printed in Mexico, 1939

Frances Toor Studios

Manchester, 8   *Mexico, D. F.*

OTHER BOOKS WRITTEN AND PUBLISHED

By Frances Toor

MEXICAN FOLKWAYS

Editor and Founder

Diego Rivera, Art Editor

(9 volumes, 1935-36)

FRANCES TOOR'S MOTORIST GUIDE TO MEXICO

SPANISH FOR YOUR MEXICAN VISIT

EASY SPANISH FOR MEXICO

SPANISH FOR YOUR MEXICAN AND CUBAN VISITS

MODERN MEXICAN ARTISTS

JOSE GUADALUPE POSADA

> A monograph of 500 reproductions from original wood and zinc cuts.   Introduction by Diego River and Frances Toor.

CANCIONERO MEXICANO

INTERPRETIVE GUIDES TO FRESCOES

THE RIVERA FRESCOES AT CUERNAVACA

FRANCES TOOR'S GUIDE TO MEXICO

Edited by McBride & Company

TO MY MOTHER

PREFACE

A few years ago I devoted a special number of my Magazine, Mexican Folkways, to the popular arts. It filled a need and sold out completely. This book is a partial substitute; it contains more material, more illustrations and will do greater justice to this vast fascinating field. But to do it full justice would take volumes, so at best it can only be an introduction.

I hope, however, to make this a genuine introduction, one that will help my readers to understand the craftsmen; to recognize their best creations and to realize the problems they are now facing. In Mexico, a country of great contrasts and paradoxes, the very poorest of the population have the time to create beautiful things for their own daily use a luxury which only the well-to-do can afford in industrialized countries.

If it is true that "Man cannot live by bread alone, it is equally true that he cannot live by beauty alone—bread and beauty is the ideal.

At the present time the beauty of the Mexican popular arts is in danger, due to the tremendously increased demand for them. Strangely enough the craftsmen are not greatly benefited; they are not receiving sufficient bread in return for the beauty they produce. On the contrary, they are the losers, for in the necessary speeding up to fill orders, their work becomes mechanized and joyless.

My hope is that this book will inspire the purchasers of the popular arts to demand good workmanship and good taste; that all those who are interested will do something to conserve these two qualities and at the same time help to improve the situation of the artist craftsmen.

Whatever success I may achieve will be due in a large measure to the many friends who have contributed directly and indirectly—Diego Rivera, Dr. Moises Saenz, Miguel Covarrubias, Count René d'Harnoncourt, Fred Davis, Roberto Montenegro, Dr. Atl, Jorge Encise, Fred Liebig, Ernesto Cervantes, Humberto Arellano, Miguel Calderón and the Indian artists craftsmen themselves.

CONTENTS

INTRODUCTION

The Mexican popular arts are among the most varied and beautiful in the world. Even though they are produced for utility, practically every object, no matter how humble and inexpensive, is touched with beauty.

Mexicans are a race of artists, especially the Indians. They have lived in poverty and in virtual slavery for centuries, yet one sees in their lives an artistic order and a love for beauty and color.

In a Mexican market everything is arranged with attention to color and design—flowers, fruit, vegetables, candles and so forth. The poorest Indian will spend his last *centavo* on a flower for his household saint, for whom his offerings are always colorful.

And the Indians seem to have a feeling for beauty, deeper than that which appeals merely to the eye. Unlike us of the so-called civilized world, they adorn objects without any desire to exhibit them. Women wear lovely handwoven sashes so twisted around their waists that the designs cannot be discerned. Ragged Otomi men carry their food and commerce in beautifully handwoven and embroidered cloths and bags. One day in a railroad station I asked one of them to show me his bag. He did so politely, but when I offered to purchase it, he said:, "No, *señorita,* it's for use."

The Mexican Indian has never divorced beauty from utility. So even now the craftsman is also an artist, as before the Conquest. In those days art was an integral part of the daily lives of all the people. Now only the well-to-do can afford it, or the poor who are able to produce it for themselves, because their time is worth so little money—as in the case of these Mexican Indians.

Over half of Mexico's population is Indian, living in an agricultural, handcraft, semi-folkloric state of civilization. It is only during the last fifteen years that the Mexican Government began to construct paved highways. Now there are hundreds of miles of them, connecting what were previously inaccessible villages with cities. But there are still innumerable villages that can only be reached over difficult mountain paths, into which machines of any kind have never entered and very few machine-made objects.

Among the Indians before the Conquest (1521) were great architects, sculptors and painters. There were also splendid craftsmen and popular artists who wrought beautiful jewels, wove fine cloth, fashioned pottery lovely in form and decoration, made exquisite humming bird feather capes, shields, mosaics and other objects.

These artists and craftsmen belonged to numerous races, the most outstanding for their art being the Tarascans, Toltec, Totonac, Zapotec, Mixtec, Maya and Aztec —the last in power at the time of the Conquest.

Immediately after the Conquest theSpaniards began proselytizing the Indians. In their attempt to impose upon them their religion, language and social forms, they cruelly and ruthlessly destroyed everything that might remind them of their past —magnificent pyramids and temples, expressive sculptures of dieties and beautifully painted picture documents. Recent excavations and studies have revealed the fact that it was a great loss to history and art.

A small percentage of the Indians grasped the meaning of the new faith and became good Christians. The majority had Christianity forced upon them and continued worshipping their pagan gods in secret and clinging to their old customs and traditions, as they are still doing to a great extent. But whether or not they believed in the Christian saints, they were forced to construct and decorate churches for them, often on the very ruins of the temples of the gods they knew and trusted. Yet the Indian artists were not permitted to paint pictures for these churches. An ordinance forbade them the fine arts for many generations.

Spaniards introduce
pottery-glazing, iron
+ leather work, glass
blowing + new
materials + processes

sculptures of deities
and Painted
Picture documents
Made them construct
+ decorate churches

to impose their
religion, language
& social standards
on Mexicans, the
Spaniards destroyed
everything that
would remind
them of their past-
pyramids, temples,

It was both impossible and impractical, however, for the Spaniards to interfere with the Indian production of articles of prime necessity, supplied by weavers, potters and other craftsmen. These could not be imported easily and there were no Spanish artisans to compete. So the Indians were permitted to continue their popular arts, among which were some un-

known to the Spaniards, such as lacquer and feather work.

The Spaniards were amazed and fascinated with the quality and beauty of the Indian handcrafts. They themselves created new demands and were able to contribute something to their enrichment in the form of new materials and processes. They introduced into Mexico iron, steel and wool, and taught the Indians pottery-glazing, iron and leather work, glass-blowing and so forth. The Spaniards also brought with them the upright loom and potter's wheel.

The strong inherent artistic sense of the Indian, however, together with his natural intelligence and skill, made it possible for him to use the new materials and methods without loss of his own artistic individuality. It is because of this that everything the Spaniards have introduced into Mexico in the fine arts, handcrafts, music, dances and so forth, has taken on a Mexican character. The Indian artist does not imitate; he transforms. The result is a Mexican art—a combination of primitive Indian with Spanish and European elements.

The handcrafts, like other commodities, have been influenced in their development by the economic forces of supply and demand.

Immediately after the Conquest, when practically all the Indian nobles were either killed or reduced to slavery, there was less demand for the finer things. It was not until the 18th. and 19th. centuries, when the wealth of the Mexican mines created a new aristocracy of Spaniards principally, that the popular arts reached their highest perfection. The decline began when it was possible to import competing objects—jewelry, dishes, glassware and others, from foreign countries.

For a long time only the wealthy could afford imported things. But recently the importation of cheap German and Japanese toys, jewelry and other objects, are making them available to the poor classes as well, especially those of the cities. The bad taste of these imported things is a demoralizing influence. Fortunately, the Indians in most of the villages have not been contaminated. They continue to produce and to like beautiful things.

At no time after the Conquest, even when the Indians, artistic production was at its best, were Indian artists or their arts respected by the higher Mexican social classes. Imported objects of inferior taste and quality were valued more highly than the finest native arts. This was especially true during the long Diaz dictatorship, when everything foreign in all the arts was admired and badly imitated, while the Mexican splendid art manifestations were looked upon with indifference.

It was not until after the 1910-20 Revolution, that the Mexican governing classes began to appreciate their own art and artists. And it was the group of modern artists, whose work has made Mexican art world famous, who were responsible for the impulse given by the Government to the fine and popular arts. These artists, instead of looking abroad for subject matter and inspiration, found the real sources for their art in their own country. Their influence grew and extended. The worthless system of teaching art in the public schools was changed. The children were no longer required to copy foreign chromos. Instead they were taught to see the beauty in their own arts and environment. They were also taught Mexican folk songs and dances, which soon found a place on festival and theater programs. A great wave of nationalism swept the country and all the Mexican arts acquired a new dignity in the eyes of Mexicans.

In 1921-2, a splendid exhibition of popular art was patronized by the Ministry of Commerce, Industry and Labor. It was organized by a group of artists, who collected objects from all over the Republic. I had just come to Mexico City, to attend the National University Summer School, when it was shown there and the beauty of it was one of the motivating factors in my remaining. I wanted to kno wmore of the country in which such humble people could make such beautiful things.

This exhibition was a revelation to the Mexicans themselves. Since then it has become quite the mode among the well-to-do Mexican families, especially those connected with the Government, to have a Mexican Room, decorated with the Indian handcrafts.

Courtesy, Dr. Atl

One of the exhibition rooms of the 1920-21 Popular art exhibition. Mexico City

In connection with this exhibition, the same Ministry published two beautifully illustrated volumes on the popular arts, entitled, "Las Artes Populares," by Dr. Atl

About ten years later, Count Rene d'Harnoncourt organized another excellent popular art exhibition, patronized by the late Ambassador Morrow, which toured the principal cities of the U. S. A. He was at that time with Fred Davis, in the Sonora News Art Shop, and both he and Mr. Davis were instrumental in having Olinala artists renew some of the fine old lacquer designs.

Since this last exhibition the Mexican handcrafts have acquired an amazing popularity. It has come with the enormous increase in the number of U. S. tourists coming to Mexico. They take them back literally by the carload. As a result innumerable popular art shops have been established in the larger cities, situated in tourist centers and the production has grown by leaps and bounds.

But the demand for the Mexican handcrafts in the U. S. has not stopped with the tourists. At first small shops were opened there and now the largest and most important department stores are carrying them. Thus within the last few years, the export end alone of this business has increased from something like ten thousand to as many millions of pesos a year.

This enormous growth in the volume of business in the popular arts must of necessity have its effects on both the craftsmen and the crafts. One unacquainted with the facts, would immediately jump at the conclusion that the craftsmen were the first to be benefited, but that is true to a limited extent only. The Mexican Indian has never been a good bargainer. As a common or skilled laborer his wages have been notoriously low. Generally an artist craftsman earns less than a common laborer. He has no union to support him and the individual craftsman is not considered in the Minimum Wage Law. As a business man the Indian craftsman is also a failure. His earnings have always been so low, that he does not know the value of time in a hand-made object, and is glad to obtain a little above the cost of his raw materials. It is true that the greater demand for the handcrafts means a more rapid turnover for those who work for themselves and steadier employment for those who work in shops, but in the last analysis their only gain is an opportunity to work harder and less happily. They are not much better off economically. In larger quantities the handcrafts sell cheaper, so their profits are not sufficient to improve their standard of living. And in larger quantities, the necessity of having to make many pieces of the same kind and often having to rush them, kills the joy of creation for the artist.

On the crafts, the effects of this incrased demand is both good and bad. Some dealers exact excellent workmanship and taste and are considerate of the craftsmen. Others care for profit only and accept orders for objects, which are neither *popular nor art:* as for example, luncheon plates with three divisions, with a cactus in one, a burro in another and the calendar stone in the third. When the new things that are constantly being made for city people are left to the taste of the artist craftsmen, they, at least, have artistic merit. But, unfortunately, only too often outsiders dictate the designs for the decorations.

If action is not taken soon to conserve the beautiful old designs and splendid techniques, after a while the Mexican handcrafts will become just so many mechanized handmade objects. This danger, however, is not imminent. There are many conscientious persons in the government and among the dealers, who are aware of these conditions. Measures are already under consideration and something will be done in the near future for both the crafts and the craftsmen.

Mexico's present problems with the handcrafts are not new. Other countries have had to face them and in some they have been solved by government intervention. Denmark has succeeded in conserving a high standard in the handcrafts and they bring high prices. In the Southwest of the United States, where conditions are exactly like our own, a committee, of which Count Rene d'Harnoncourt is chairman, appointed by the Federal Bureau of Indian Affairs, is working on plans for saving the Indian handcrafts. Recent information is to the effect that they are meeting with success.

If other countries have been able to save their handcrafts from degenerating, Mexico has even a better opportunity. In Mexico the handcrafts are a tradition and an economic necessity, and the Indians are accustomed to beauty in form and decoration.

Often I have heard foreigners in Mexico express the regret that the country was becoming too modern and that soon there would be no more popular arts. It is true that Mexico is progressing and that some day machine-made objects will substitute many of the handcrafts, thus saving the energy of the craftsmen for more lucrative work. But even then there will be artist craftsmen in whom the creative urge will live on. If we appreciate them sufficiently, there will always be beautiful handmade things in Mexico.

Courtesy, Lola Martínez de Alvarez Bravo

HOW THE INDIAN ARTIST CRAFTSMEN LIVE AND WORK

Descendants of all the races that existed at the time of the Conquest are living today in practically the same geographical areas, speaking the Indian tongues and conserving many of the ancient customs of their ancestors. Among them, in almost every village, are some artist craftsmen. In some nearly all the inhabitants devote themselves to one or to several related crafts. But whether a few or many artists live in anyone village or town, they enjoy no special distinction, as in our modern communities

No Indian thinks that his neighbor has a special gift from the gods just because he can form a lovely clay bowl or paint a gourd beautifully. He will admire them and say, "Qué bonito!" But he knows that he, too, could do similar things or others equally lovely had his father or someone else taught him. So our artist craftsman is just an ordinary individual in his community, who lives, works and behaves like everyone else. If he happens to be an outstanding personality, meriting special respect, it is for reasons aside from his artistic talents.

An Indian's material equipment is very simple and primitive. He lives in a hut barren of practically all furniture. In some instances the Indians have so far accepted modern ways of living as to use tables, chairs and beds. The majority, however, still  sleep on the ground on *petates* or handwoven reed mats, like those used before the Conquest, and eat squatting around the *tlaquil*, the ancient Indian stove. Food is so simple that pottery mugs, bowls and pots suffice for dishes and kitchen utensils. The fingers with the help of the tortilla (a thin, unleavened maize pancake, which takes the place of bread), serve for forks and spoons. Indians who have a little money have houses consisting of several huts, around a patio, forming a compound, but the furnishings are generally like those of their poorer neighbors.

Clothing is more complicated and affords a greater opportunity for display of opulence. There are many regional styles, which will be discussed in detail in other parts of the book.

Men wear thick unbleached cotton suits. There is very little noticeable difference in the cut of the trousers, but a great variety in the shirts. Sometimes they are plaited and sometimes plain. Often they are of a different color from the trousers—pink, yellow, rose-color, blue, orange. The shirts are worn either hanging outside or with the ends tied in front or caught in at the waist or inside, with a wide handwoven sash or belt of some kind. For protection against the cold, they use sarapes, never overcoats They always wear sombreros and generally *guaraches*, although many still go barefoot. Indians who work in factories or on road construction nearly all wear blue overalls.

In some regions women still use blouses in the pre-Conquets stylelong or short *huipiles* and *quezquematl*; also the *enagua* or skirt, consisting of many yards of handwoven wool cloth, laid in plaits around the waist and held on by one wide or several narrow sashes. As a rule, however, they wear the long full calico skirt, with a wide ruffle at the bottom. With these go full waists of the same material, hanging outside of the skirt or white shirts embroidered around the neck and arms, which are worn inside with belts. Children, young girls and women all use the *rebozo* or long narrow shawl for both coat and hat. They all adorn themselves with many strings of colored beads and fantastic silver earrings. When they can afford it, they prefer gold earrings and chains. They love color, so nearly always wear bright ribbons in their black braids.

Indians of both sexes are good looking, walk with easy natural grace and wear their clothes with style. There is much individuality and élegance expressed in the tilt of a sombrero, the way a sarape is flung over the shoulders of a man, and charm in the numerous inimitable ways the women have of draping their *rebozos* over their heads and shoulders. No matter how poorly dressed some Indians may be, they are never abashed in the presence of city people. They nearly always carry themselves with dignity and are ceremoniously polite.

With some few exceptions, the Indians' tools and implements are as simple and primitive as the furnishings of their huts. They usually work hard and their hours are always long.

Even when they take time off for festivals or trips to markets, they work hard, for they walk long distances and carry heavy loads.

The artist craftsmen must work leisurely in order to produce worth-while objects. The pleasure and pride they take in their work is evident in the way they decorate even the inexpensive things they make for themselves. Their toys, miniature figures, masks and so forth express a strong sense of humor and joy in craftsmanship. The Spanish idiom that we use to express this is to say that they work with affection — *Trabajan con cariño*.

Generally an entire family work at the same craft and there is a division of labor, men and boys doing certain tasks, women and girls others. Much of the work is done out of doors and one does not think of occupational diseases in connection with handcrafts. Yet weavers who use the upright looms, often placed in dark airless huts and others working under unfavorable conditions for long hours, develop chronic and dangerous diseases of various kinds.

Not all the crafts afford steady all-year employment, and even when they do there are many interruptions. The village governments demand community tasks, such as repairs and construction of public buildings and roads, police duty and others. There are also many secular and religious holidays —festivals to the patron and other saints of one's own and neighboring villages and long pilgrimages to the shrines of very miraculous saints. In addition, there are the family saint's or birthdays, weddings, baptisms and other affairs to celebrate.

Even though all these festivals take a great deal of time and make heavy inroads into the meager year's earnings, they are welcome breaks in what would otherwise be a round of continuous work and dull living. For the craftsman, especially, they afford a valuable opporunity for new ideas and inspiration.

Often an Indian artist takes time off to do nothing at all. He will sit for hours without moving and the observer who lacks understanding and sympathy will say he is lazy. But when he returns to his work, the result is a beautiful object.

Courtesy, Friedrich Liebig

POPULAR ART STATES, MARKETS AND STORES

Most of the popular arts of today are produced by the same races (no longer pure, of course) and in the same regions that were noted for their arts before the Conquest. Taking them in the order in which they are mentioned in the Introduction and without attempting to be exact—the Tarascans lived in the section of the country now known as the States of Michoacan and Jalisco; the Toltec (a highly civilized and artistic race, disappeared long before the Conquest) in Puebla, Hidalgo and Mexico; the Zapotec and Mixtec in Oaxaca; the Totonac, in Veracruz; the Maya, in Yucatan; the Aztec in all the States of the Central Plateau and in many others.

All these states have magnificient archaeological monuments, splendid colonial cities, good climates and very beautiful scenery. As a result they are the most populated and attract the greatest number of tourists. But even though in a lesser degree, the remaining states are also interesting because of one or of several of the above mentioned attributes, as well as for beautiful handmade objects.

Handcraft villages and markets are to be found everywhere. Although some of them can be reached only over difficult mountain trails, many may be visited comfortably by rail or in car over good roads.

Almost all popular arts not specially ordered by a dealer reach some market. The market, in Aztec *tianguis,* is a pre-Conquest institution and continues to be an important factor in the lives of the Indians, both because of its commercial and social possibilities.

In villages and small towns the market is generally held on specified days on the central plaza, but in the larger towns and cities there is one or several market places, with a daily market in a permanent building. There are always booths and venders in the plaza and streets surrounding these buildings, and on special days they extend over a much greater area, sometimes covering many blocks. As a protection against the sun, vendors often set up poles to hold pieces of coarse cotton cloth, that give the appearance of white umbrellas or open tents, which with the dark people moving under them create a very oriental and picturesque effect.

Markets are held at least once or twice a week in every village, town and city and also in connection with every small and large festival. A Mexican festival is an art in itself and the market is an integral part of the festival.

Indians attend markets to barter, sell, buy; to meet old acquaintances and to make new ones. They walk for days to markets, carrying heavy loads. When they are going to a festival market which may last for days or a week, often the entire family travel together, with all their household goods. Arriving there, they set up housekeeping and live as in their own homes and are happy in the social life of their environment. Nothing is lacking and everything is very gay. The church with its saints is always nearby; there are religious dances and sometimes plays; there may even be social dancing; at night gorgeous fireworks; vendors of ballads and songs sing their wares, Besides there are people from so many places to exchange news and wares with.

An oft repeated but significant joke expressing the Indian's pleasure in being at the market is to the effect that an American met a craftsman on the way to a market and offered to purchase the few things he was taking there. The Indian refused the offer, saying, "What shall I do there all day long without anything to sell?"

On market days roads leading to the places where they are being held are throbbingly alive with people and animals. They are a strange sight in this 20th century, especially when walking along a modern highway. Men carry huge crates of pottery or rolls of *petates* on their backs, hanging from a strap from the forehead in pre-Conquest fashion. Burros are so laden that often only their thin legs and funnily cut tails are visible. Sometimes a mother with a baby slung in a *rebozo* on her back and several children ride a burro, from whose sides are hanging full baskets. Sometimes the man asserts his superiority by riding while the woman trots along side of the animal. Others walk lightly, carrying only some small package or, perhaps, just one chicken or turkey to sell. As they pass in endless procession, outlined against a background of green fields or dark woods, with here and there flashes of color from a skirt, blouse, shirt or gay sarape, watching them is an unforgettable experience.

Among the largest and most interesting of the most visited and accessible markets are Toluca (Fridays; State of Mexico); Patzcuaro (Fridays; State of Michoacán); Oaxaca (Saturdays State of Oaxaca). There are innumerable other markets, both large and small that are both interesting and picturesque, which can also be reached without any difficulty.

All markets are fascinating and great fun. It is fun just to talk with the Indians and to take part in their delightful game of selling. They begin by naming a price which they do not expect to receive. If you comment that it is too high, they answer, "But that is only the asking price; you offer—*ofrezca.* If you make an unsatisfactory offer, they continue, smiling and in a most expressive tone of voice, *Con ganas de comprar, ¿cuánto das?*— "With an honest desire to buy, how much will you give?" It is an endless game, for the bargaining can go on as long as you enjoy it. Recently, however, I have found at some markets frequented by many city people that the Indians no longer enjoy the game of bargaining, and have heard them say brusquely, "This is the price. Take it or leave it."

No matter how fascinating it may be to visit and to buy at markets, one must go to stores for variety in the popular arts. Most markets have only what is made in the vicinity and certain objects are not sold at markets because the Indians have no use for them and they are too high priced.

In the larger cities the number of well supplied popular arts and craft shops are constantly increasing. They have objects from all parts of the country, at fixed prices, which are seldom too high for value received.

In some shops excellent taste is displayed; in others the contrary is true. But in everyone of them there are some good things, because no shopkeeper who is selling Mexican hand-crafts can escape having them.

The ideal is to have only objects of good taste in all the shops. Do I hear my readers say that it is impossible to realize? I agree with them. But I know that they will agree with me that there could be a great improvement in good taste if all the purchasers of the popular arts would demand it.

Carrying petates to market

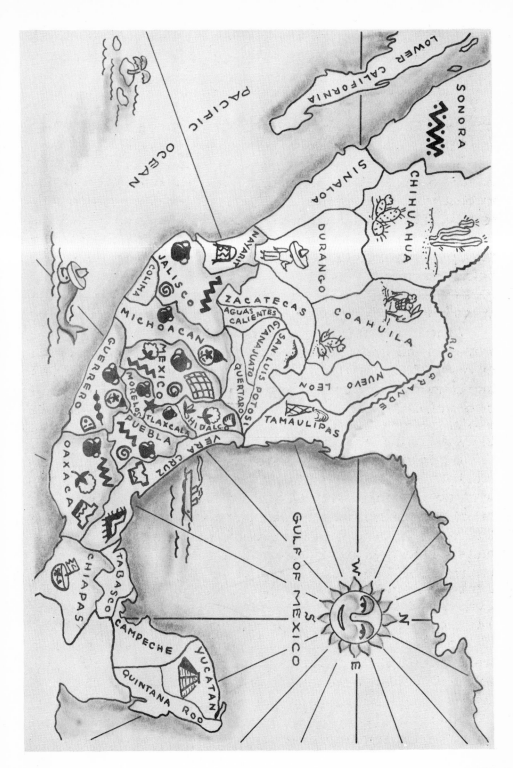

WEAVING IN WOOL AND COTTON

Weaving is one of the oldest as well as one of the most important of the Mexican handcrafts. There is sufficient evidence to believe that it began among the first Indians who came to Mexico, known as the Archaic, which according to some students was ten and to others three thousand years ago. By the time the Spaniards arrived, in 1521, this art had achieved such high perfection, that Cortes and the chroniclers of the period wrote glowing accounts of the fine cloths and magnificent garments of the Indians.

As wool was unknown before the Conquest, all fabrics were woven of the native fibres from the cotton plants, cactus and maguey. Some of these were spun into very fine and others into course threads by means of the spindle set into a clay whorl or a *malacate*. The loom was of the horizontal type, with one end of the warp tied to a post and the other on a belt encircling the waist of the weaver.

It appears from the reproductions in the codices that only one heddle was used, yet the weavers were so skillful that they were able to make the most intricate designs. They learned the art of making dyes from insects, plants and shells—scarlet from the cochineal, blue from the indigo plant, fine purple from the murex shells from along the Pacific Coast. They also obtained indescribably beautiful color patterns in their textiles by massing a great variety of feathers of the humming and of other colorful birds, such as the toucans, macaws, blue jays, scarlet tangers. The iridescent green tail plumes of the quetzal were reserved for the priesthood and the nobility. No wonder the Spaniards were dazzled by the garments of those amazingly brilliant cloths, especially when they were worn with exquisitely wrought jewels of gold and precious stones.

After the Conquest the weavers began to use the upright loom and the spinning wheel, which the Spaniards brought to

Mexico. But they never abandoned their own loom and way of spinning. They call the imported loom *telar* and their own *telar de otate*—otate being the cloth of which the belt is made. The Indians even now use the pre-Conquest spinning whorls, which have been excavated in quantities, some of them beautifully ornamented with modelled and engraved designs; or they make new ones of clay or wood after the old patterns. It is not unusual to see the Otomi Indians, of the State of Hidalgo, spinning in the ancient manner, as they sit selling their wares in the markets or are walking along the Mexico-Laredo Highway, with their burdens on their backs.

For centuries after the Conquest all cloth continued to be handwoven and colored with the natural dyes, with the difference that some of it was made of wool. It was not until the end of the 19th century, after the establishment of the first large textile mills in Mexico, that the Indians began to use machine-made cottons. But they still weave practically everything that they use in wool, and much in cotton, so that even at the present time weaving is one of the most important and widespread of the popular arts.

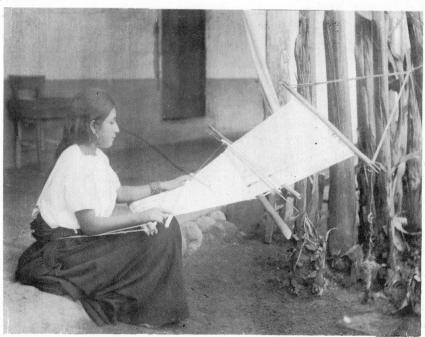

Weaving on horizontal loom, Tuxpan, Jalisco

Although the weavers of today are very skillful and some of them can make designs that are as intricate and beautiful as the ancient ones, weaving is no longer the fine art that it used to be. This is due to the competition of excellent imported wool cloth and blankets, which the moneyed classes can afford to purchase. As stated previously, during the last two decades there has been a slightly awakened interest among the city Mexicans in handwoven cloths and especially in sarapes, but in reality all that the weavers produce in those lines are either used by the Indians themselves or bought by foreigners. In any event they have to be sold cheaply, so that the weavers who supply the demands of their own markets and the constantly increasing number of stores, are no longer able to put as much time into the work as formerly. But there are still villages untouched by this new turnover in the popular arts, where the weavers work as in the ancient days.

One would expect to find the villages in which the weavers work according to the old traditions—spinning their own wool, making their own dyes and so forth, and in which the Indians use more homespuns, far away from large cities and markets. But that is not always true. There are Indians in villages, in the States of Mexico and Hidalgo, within a few hours from Mexico City by bus and near their own state Capitals, who work in the old way and use more homespun materials than others in remote mountain villages, days on horseback from any stores and large markets. These conditions are determined by the resources of their environment. There are regions in Hidalgo, altogther unsuited for agriculture but good grazing ground for sheep, and soil in which the cactus and maguey thrive, furnishing fibre for the weaving of bags, carrying cloths, string and so forth. And, too, the Indians who live there are too poor to buy anything machine-made.

Just as in the material aspects of weaving so in the others, the ancient customs are conserved. The children generally learn the trades of their parents. They work in family groups, both sexes doing the various tasks indiscriminately. Children begin by carding and spinning, when they are mere babies of five or six years old. They are also shepherds at that age and spin while they watch their flocks. At eight or nine years they start working on the looms.

Before the Conquest there was a deity that watched over the weavers. Now they have a patron saint in every shop. In the huts there is always the household saint. But if one scrapes the surface of their Catholicism, he will always find a little paganism just below. The Indians never fully rely on the saints, so they still make offerings to the elements and to natural objects. In a village in Hidalgo, where the Indians make their dyes from herbs and the bark of various trees, they take dyed strands of wool, colored paper ribbons and food to bury near the roots of some very ancient oaks. They also dress themselves in the colors they are taking and say special prayers in Aztec, so that the new dyes they are going to make may turn out well.

Upright loom and spinning wheel

SARAPES, generally of pure wool, are the showiest and most important of the handwoven objects. They are worn by men and boys only, for whom they serve as overcoats, for adornment, as wedding cloaks and in the end for shrouds. The same sarapes are used for covers at night, to spread things upon in the market place and to stretch over poles for shelter in the open.

Before the Conquest men wore flowing capes of varying lengths, tied either in front or over the right shoulder, called *tilmas* in Aztec. The sarape, a substitute for these, is a much more practical garment. The large ones are about the size and shape of an ordinary blanket, sometimes of one but usually of two pieces, sewed together in the middle with wool of the same color so that it is not noticeable. There is an opening in the center sufficiently large to slip over the head, called a *bocamanga*, which name also extends to the diamond-shaped design around it.

There are small sarapes that are worn over the shoulders, reaching to or below the waist, called *cotones* or *tilmas*. Some of them are of cotton and some of cotton and wool; white background with colored stripes. There are also medium-sized ones of wool, called *jorongos*. In Colima and Jalisco, they are of red wool, and as it is always warm there in the day time, they are folded and worn over the left shoulder for adornment. The full-sized sarapes, when used for protection against the cold, are flung around the shoulders with a dignity which transforms the poorest Indian into a fine noble figure.

Sarapes are woven everywhere, generally on upright looms by men, and everywhere they are different. Even in sarape-weaving villages that supply markets and stores, where many weavers use the same colors and designs, no two are exactly alike. Every weaver expresses his own personality in his work. Yet because of their similarity, one with experience can recognize the regions they are from.

San Miguel de Chicumuac, near Texcoco, Mexico, is one of the well known sarape weaving centers. The typical ones from there are of a heavy firm weave, blue blackground, with black and white geometrical border designs and *bocamanga*, with here and there a touch of red. Other colors are also used,

Showing a variety of Texcoco designs, two with diamond-shaped Bocamanga

but the texture and decorative motifs are generally the same. Villages around Toluca—Guadalupita, Metepec and others, produce lighter-weight sarapes, of looser weave, usually in natural wool colors, with all-over designs.

An outstanding sarape-weaving village of Puebla, is Santa Ana Chautempan. Here the designs are similar to those of Texcoco, but of different colors, crosswise stripes, finer weave and lighter weight. White sarapes with pleasing borders and centers of red flowers are also woven there. Now they are producing new patterns for tourists, with colors that shriek to the heavens, and they sell.

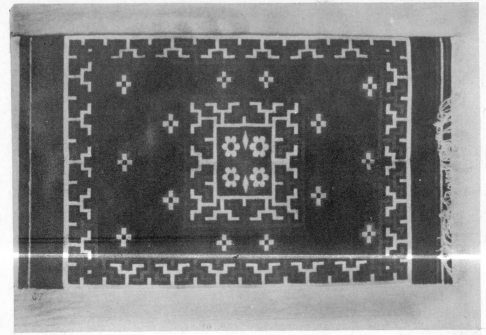

Santa Ana Chautenpan sarape

From Teotitlan del Valle, the village that supplies the Oaxaca City stores and large markets, come light-weight, loosely-woven sarapes with stylized animal designs in the center, on soft grey wool, with white and black striped borders; others have a black or red center, with flags or flowers at the sides; some are of pleasing blue and black designs on a white background. Here, also, they have a tourist specialty of bright colors, with designs of idols or calendar stones.

Around Patzcuaro, Michoacan and Silao and Dolores, Guanajuato, the sarapes are of dark colors, coarse weave, with very simple but pleasing red designs. In Jocotepec, near Guadalajara, the weavers make very handsome sarapes, of dark natural wool colors, with border and center designs of red flowers. The Mayo Indians, of Sonora, weave a rough one-piece sarape, white background, with lovely blue, black and brown decorative motifs. From around San Luis Potosi and Aguascalientes come the very fine, tightly woven sarapes, with all-over polichrome patterns of cross-wise stripes, the kind Mexican charros love to sport

In San Miguel Allende, Guanajuato, in this same region, where sarapes were once made that competed with the fine old ones of Saltillo, the weavers still produce good, heavy ones, of natural wool colors, but mostly for home consumption.

Sarapes of soft weave, with little design, used for bed covers, are called *frazadas* or *cobijas*. In some villages around Toluca, the Indians make bed covers, which they call *sábanas*, of white wool, and embroider them in handsome cross-stitch contrasting colored wool stylized designs of animals and flowers.

There are innumerable styles of sarapes that are scarcely ever seen excepting on the back of some Indian, of beautiful texture and very simple adornment; the kind that are made solely for home consumption. Notable among these are the Tarahumara sarapes, heavy and roughly woven, of either white or dark natural wool colors, which have that peculiar beauty derived only from texture and simplicity.

Mayo sarapes from the state of Sonora

William P. Spratling, of Taxco, has revived many fine old sarape designs. His weavers spin their own wool and make their own dyes, so that his sarapes have the feel and beauty of the genuine old ones. Artes de Mexico, Mexico City, are weaving sarapes in which they reproduce the Toluca and Maya Indian designs.

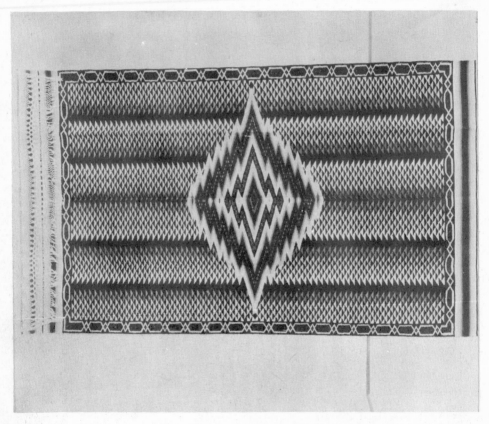

A fine old San Miguel Allende Sarape

There are still hidden away in ancient family chests some of the highly treasured, exquisitely fine and beautiful century-old Saltillo sarapes. Occasionally one may be bought at a very high price. In comparison those made now seem inferior. Yet there are a sufficient number among the new ones, produced in such huge quantities, to demonstrate the fact that the weavers of today are not only excellent craftsmen but also artists.

Courtesy, Lola Martínez de Alvarez Bravo

HANDWOVEN CLOTH is not in very great demand, yet there are nice wool and cotton homespuns made everywhere by men and women on both the horizontal and upright looms. A specialty in Oaxaca for city people is a great variety of cotton, dinner, tea and bridge sets, in plain or combined colors, embroidered with birds and small idols. There are also aprons of the same type. Celaya, Guanajuato, is another weaving center for table cloths and napkins, but they are for regional consumption. Wool cloth for city stores and markets comes from Santa Ana, Puebla; Leon, Guanajuato; Guadalajara, Jalisco, and other places, and it is either plain, striped or checked. In almost every sarape-weaving village and others, Indians weave cloth for their own use, nicer than that found in shops. Popular art stores do not specialize in homespuns, yet they all carry the Oaxaca table sets. Artes de México, Mexico City, have a very fine line of wool and cotton homespuns, of good texture and attractive designs, much of it made by their own weavers.

SASHES (In Spanish *fajas* or *ceñidores*), of cotton and wool, are worn as well as woven by both men and women, but mostly by the latter. They vary from one and a half to five inches in width and from one to five yards in length, and are different in every region. Most of the cotton sashes are wide, of plain colors and worn by men. The Otomíes of Hidalgo, however, weave very fine ornate cotton ones. Around Toluca, the Otomíes make theirs of wool with very pleasing designs. In Milpa Alta, Mexico, the Aztec women use narrow and wide sashes, cotton backs with charming inwoven wool designs, of stylized birds, flowers and butterflies. In the Sierras of Oaxaca, the sashes are of wool and narrow, not very ornate but of good texture; in Chiapas they are plain and coarsely woven. Women from around Patzcuaro use several narrow wool sashes of different colors and designs at the same time. Huichol men wear long wide, brown wool sashes, lovely in texture, with simple beautiful geometrical designs.

First sash to the left, huichol: remaining ones from Michoacan

WOOLEN BAG FROM IXMIQUILPAN HIDALGO.

WOOL BAGS (*bolsas* or *morrales* in Spanish) are not used so commonly as those made of fibre. In Ixmiquilpan and Zimapan, Hidalgo, the Otomíes make very beautiful wool bags, of various sizes and colors, with inwoven designs of stylized birds, animals and flowers for ordinary practical use. Other tribes that specialize in them are the Cora and Huichol Indians, of Nayarit. Their bags are smaller but with very lovely geometrical designs. Huichol men use tiny bags on a string around the waist for adornment.

REBOZO, the Mexican woman's shawl, apparently had no counterpart before the Conquest. It seems to have been introduced by the Spaniards and to have grown out of the necessity that a woman cover her head with something soft in the Christian temples. No Mexican woman of any class ever wears a hat in church.

The rebozo is of the same importance to the woman as the sarape is to the man. It is her coat and hat; serves as a cradle for the baby on her back and blanket when it is lying beside her; for a market basket; as a cover for a large clay pot of tamales on the street; the fringe twisted on the head, as a stand for a basket or water jar. Often young girls wear rebozos folded on the shoulders and crossed in front for adornment.

Rebozos for adults are about a yard wide by two and a half long, including the fringe. Smaller ones are made for children. They are generally woven on horizontal looms by both sexes, the women making the intricate fringe. As they are a garment for the poor, nearly all rebozos are of ordinary cotton thread and conservative colors—dark-blues, greys, browns, with fine white pin-point, all-over designs. These designs are achieved in the dyeing and require great skill. The weavers take balls of white cotton thread and form skeins with the help of a wheel. Then they tie the thread at certain points, so that it does not take the dye, thus forming the designs.

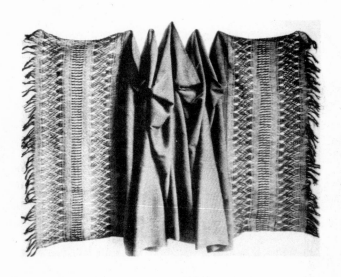

As most of the rebozos have the pin-point designs, the regional differences are very subtle, with the exception of those of Michoacan and thereabouts, which are of plain dark blue background, with a wide white lengthwise stripe, bright colored fringe sometimes adorned with feathers. Occasionally rebozos are woven of silk or rayon in brighter colors, with the pin-point designs, which are used for holidays.

The finest and loveliest of all the rebozos, however, are of such fine thread that they can be pulled through a ring. These are of the usual pin-point designs and are called *rebozos de bolita*. They are seldom made now, but there are many old ones in existence from the famous sarape-weaving villages of Santa Maria, San Luis Potosi, and Tenancingo, Mexico.

Such an important garment as the rebozo is woven everywhere. There are, however, many well-known rebozo-weaving centers, such as those mentioned above. Others are: Texcoco, Mexico; Leon, Guanajuato; Paracho, Michoacan, and Guadalajara, Jalisco.

Courtesy, Fred Davis

Rebozo with rose design, Puebla: the other Santa
María, San Luis Potosí

As the rebozo does not interest city people nor foreigners to any great extent, it has not changed much. I have, however, recently seen rebozos in Patzcuaro with the word Michoacan woven into the fringe, showing that it has not entirely escaped tourist influence. It remains, nevertheless, a typical folk garment. Young girls know how to make it enhance their charm and coquetishness and women their dignity. A group of them in rebozos is a beautiful picture.

Showing typical way of wearing rebozo in Oaxaca

WEAVING IN REED, PALM AND FIBRE

PETATES (Aztec for reed mats) are as primitive and their use as widespread as before the Conquest. They are handwoven —the coarse ones of a reed, called *tule*; the finer ones of palm.

Most Indians sleep on the ground and the pétate serves as both bed and mattress; when the bed is improvised of boards or sticks, the petate is the mattress. The Indian comes into the world on a petate and leaves it rolled in one, for often, it serves as a coffin. On November 2nd, when the dead are expected to return to partake of their favorite dishes in spirit, the food is placed on a new petate. In markets, foods, toys, fruit and all sorts of other things are spread on petates. Gifts for festivals and weddings are received on petates. It is the bridal bed and in Tuxpan, Jalisco, a new petate is carried to church by one of the bridal party.

Generally petates are the size of a sarape or a double bed, but there are smaller and larger ones and some are in strips like floor runners. They are made wherever tule and palms grow and sold everywhere at very low prices. The finer palm petates come from Puebla, Guerrero and Oaxaca, where they are decorated with geometrical designs in reds, blues yellows and violet and cost more than those made of Tule. The tule petates are ·never dyed; are of simple designs and coarsely woven.

The Lerma River and lagoons in the Toluca region furnish much tule and many petates are made there. The Indians also make amusing and interesting petate figures of soldiers, horses and animals and charming birds and rattles and all sorts of toys. Similar toys, birds and rattles are also made of the palm petate and in addition large purses that fit into each other that serve for sewing baskets and small purses; also a low round basket, shaped like a vase, called a *tompeate*. Plain round baskets are made of tule petate, as well as special ones for tortillas, known as *chiquihuites* in Aztec. Due to the softness and flexibility of the petate, much of it is used for packing.

The important and intimate character of the petate has given rise to a number of popular sayings in connection with it. To describe an undertaking started with great enthusiasm and then suddenly dropped—"Llamarada de petate" or "Petate flame".— Instead of saying a person has died, the noun is changed into a verb—"Se petateó," meaning that he took himself off in a petate. "Ya lió su petate"—"He has tied up his petate," means that a person has left the place. To indicate that a person is of lower rank than yourself—"De esas pulgas no brincan en mi petate" or Those fleas do not jump on my petate," "El que nace en un petate siempre anda erutando a tule"—He who was born on a petate always belches tule" is a figurative way of describing a vulgar person, and so on.

This picture shows a variety of petate toys from the state of Mexico. They make many others there as well as huge military figures and persons and saints.

The Petate man

Courtesy, Luis Marquez

SOMBREROS are a very common article. They are hand woven, of palm, in all textures, shapes and sizes. Every body in the Indian male world wears them and occasionally a woman will use one instead of a *rebozo* for protection against the sun.

Sombreros are made everywhere and everywhere they are different, the differences being found in the shape and size of both crown and brim. Sometimes they are adorned with a finely woven horsehair, leather or braid band. The finest sombreros come from Yucatan, Chiapas and especially Tabasco, where they are of normal size. In Morelos the crowns are fairly large and the brims so wide, that often the wearer has to take his hat off or to tip it in order to be able to enter an ordinary doorway. The Indians from Papantla, Veracruz, wear hats with small brims and very tall crowns. The shape of the sombreros of the Huichol Indians, of Nayarit, resembles that of the Chinese—no crowns and the brims of ordinary size, often adorned with tropical bird feathers or colored bands of wool.

SOMBREROS DE PALMA
MEXICO. 188.

Sombreros from everywhere

BASKETS are the products of agricultural peoples, hence they are among the oldest of the Mexican handcrafts.

In baskets, as well as in the other popular arts, there are regional differences. Those of San Juan del Rio, Queretaro, are well known. They are of the natural color of the palm, beautifully woven, with a brown band near the top. Among the most popular are the Toluca baskets, made in the Village of Santa Ana, just of the Toluca Highway and elsewhere. The palm is dyed in a great variety of colors and then woven into designs of animals and figures. They are made in all sizes and shapes, with and without covers—for clothes, sewing, paper and so forth.

Toluca baskets

Luis Marquez

FIBRE of a squat maguey is spun and made into rope and string The Otomi Indians of Hidalgo, weave *ayates* or carrying cloths of this fibre on horizontal looms. Some of these are coarsely woven and others so fine that they could be used for curtains. Sometimes they are embroidered in bright wool colors. Around Toluca the ayates are heavier, of tighter weave and richly embroidered in bands of stylized animals, birds and flowers. The finest ones are used for altar cloths and for carrying flowers and candles on pilgrimages to festivals.

There are many other ways in which the materials described above are utilized. A handful of fibre or (estropajo), is used instead of a wash-cloth or for scrubbing. The b o t t o m s of chairs or benches are woven of tule. A picturesque rain cape worn by the Indians is.made of palm leaves. and it is really rain-proof:

Hammocks woven or palm or *ixtli*, maguey fibre, are used a great deal in Tierra Caliente or the hot regions of the country, often serving as beds. Oaxaca Indians make an unusually attractive fibre bag, called a *red* or net, because of the weave. It is in two sections—the lower one pointed and closely woven; the upper composed of long loosely woven, gayly colored bands of purple, blue ceris, yellow and the undyed ixtli. It is closed with strong narrow fibre band, drawn through loops, which is also attached to the point at the bottom, so that the bag may be slung from the shoulder or hung from a saddle. Guerrero produces fine palm hammocks, as well as colorful mats to put under saddles. Some Yucatan hammocks are made of henequen and the finer ones. of cotton thread, frequently mixed with rayon. The henequen fibre serves for rope and other purposes. Sometimes the Indians make their entire guaraches, even the soles, of fibre. In Puebla the dead are buried in crude ixtli guaraches, made especially for the purpose.

EMBROIDERY — DRAWNWORK — CROCHETING — KNITTING — BEADING

EMBROIDERY before the Conquest went together with weaving and was under the same Aztec Goddess, Xochiquetzal. Since then it has been enriched by new materials and designs and is very popular down to the present time.

Indians embroider shirts, skirts, covers, napkins, bags and aprons, and do very beautiful work. Women and gils of all social classes embroider in Mexico, but there is less utility and beauty in their work than in the Indians'

They do solid and cross-stitch embroidery, with foreign and Indian motifs. There are some very fine old samplers.

In Almoloya del Rio, Mexico, in the Toluca region, the Indians make tea and bridge sets, bags and center pieces of unbleached cotton and embroider them with silk in attractive designs. These things are sold in the markets of that vicinity and in city stores.

Mexican women, among them Indians, do the exquisite and marvelously beautiful embroidery in gold, silver and silk on the church vestments and very elegant bullfighter's costumes.

DRAWNWORK is done everywhere but there are centers where it is a specialty, as in Aguascalientes and Irapuato, Guanajuato. They make center pieces, doilies, handkerchiefs and other things and do very fine work. It is, however, unfortunate that the materials they work on are not so fine. Mexico does not produce linen. City stores often buy imported linen and have the women make handkerchiefs, napkins and table cloths.

CROCHETING and KNITTING is done by the Indians but never for their own use. In these lines as well as in others they do good work. One sees men on the streets of Mexico City, selling knitted sweaters and sox, and while they are waiting for people to buy they are knitting.

BEADING Fine bead designs on cloths, napkins, bags, cigarette cases, hat bands and so forth, were very popular in the 18th Century among city people. At the present time this type embroidery is chiefly used and done by Indian women, who adorn their shirts with lovely colorful designs, as well as handwoven hair bands, little baskets and other objects. Huicholes make beautiful bead bracelets, which the men wear. Large glass beads are used to adorn headdresses of religious dancers and are worn in strings around the neck by Indian women and girls everywhere. Colored spangle designs are used on dancers costumes and China Poblana skirts.

Embroideries and handwoven sashes from around
Toluca. Camisa from Puebla.

REGIONAL DRESS

When the Indians were masters in their own land, they dressed in colorful garments, painted their faces and wore jewels of gold and precious stones. The governing classes, nobles and priests, naturally, used more costly materials and adornments, but even the clothes of the poor were handmade and beautiful. Their centuries of poverty since the Spaniards came, have affected their present day manner of dressing. None. of them use paint any longer and they cannot afford the same quality of materials and rich adornments. Yet their dress, although impoverished and more sombre, still conserves some of the ancient dignity and picturesqueness.

It would take much more space than this book permits to point out all the regional differences, but the strikingly outstanding costumes can be described easily.

WOMEN in some villages are still using two pre-Conquest style blouses—the *quexquematl*, without sleeves, made of two straight pieces of cloth, so joined that it has two points; the *huipil*, long or short, square-necked, loose and shapless, with short sleeves. The majority wear calico waists, which hang loosely outside of the skirt or *camisas*—shirts with short sleeves, embroidered in silk or beads, belted inside of the skirt.

Enaguas or skirts are of three styles—plain pieces of cloth sewed together and folded around the waist, resembling the ·ones of the codices; woolen skirts, of many yards of cloth, which is laid in deep plaits around the waist every time they are put on, with the plaits either falling over the handwoven sashes with which they are fastened in back, like a fan (sometimes the plaits are in front). The third is the long, full calico skirt, with a deep ruffle at the bottom, just old fashioned peasant anywhere.

Aprons are also worn to a considerable extent and they are often beautifully embroidered.

Young Indian girls in cities are beginning to wear modern calico dresses, of colorful prints, which are sold in every market, at reasonable prices.

Otomi women from villages around Toluca, wear the plaited wool skirt, which they call a *chincuete,* fastened with a long wide sash. The cloth is handwoven, of dark blue or purple

background, with white pin, crosswise stripes. Their blouses are either the woolen quexquematl or the cotton camisas. Formerly it was possible to tell the village a woman came from by the color of her skirt and the width of the stripe. It still is but the majority no longer wear the chincuete and quexquematl. The Hidalgo Otomi women dress in long cotton skirts and occasionally wear a quexquematl, woven of fine dark blue thread, with white stripes, of the same texture as their sashes.

In some villages in the mountains of Puebla, women wear dark wool quexquematl, handsomely embroidered in bright wool. Totonac women of Papantla and other villages of that region, in Veracruz, due to the heat, wear white cotton quexquematl, some of them beautifully embroidered and plain skirts. Formerly the women of Papantla wore elaborately embroidered costumes, but now, unfortunately, they are using German machine-made embroideries and laces.

Huipils, always of cotton, are worn in many villages of Veracruz and Oaxaca, and in every village the materials, lengths, color and embroidery designs are different. In Veracruz the huipils are generally full length and worn without skirts, and are richly embroidered. Those of the Mixtec Mountains, in Oaxaca, are knee-length and the plain skirt is adorned with a band at the bottom that harmonizes with the embroidery around the neck and sleeves. Women of Yalalag, a village in the Sierra of Juarez, Oaxaca, use a unique huipil, of heavy white cotton homespun, with a stitched yoke and a white tassle or one of contrasting color, at the neck. The skirts are of the same material but sometimes with light brown stripes. Their headdress is most extraordinary and they are very stunning.

The Mestizas, as the Indian women of Yucatan are called, wear long white machine-made cotton huipils, embroidered in bright flower designs around the neck, sleeves and bottom. For holiday occasions the huipil is only knee-length, of silk or fine cotton, and the skirts are either embroidered in colors to match the blouse or adorned with fine lace. The Mestizas are very charming in their spotlessly white huipils, colored ribbons in their black hair and the long filagree rosaries and earrings to match.

A tehuana and a tehuano. The Xicapexli in the
background, a lacquered and painted gourd bowl,
in which the tehuanas carry fruit and flowers to
market, is decorated for the fruit-throwing fiesta

The Tehuanas or women of Tehuantepec, Oaxaca, are famous for both their picturesque dress and good looks. They wear
a waist-length huipil, of colored cloth, on occasions of silk, embroidered with flowers or adorned by machine with thread designs. Their skirts are of the old-fashioned type, of contrasting
colors, with a wide white flounce at the bottom. They use colored ribbons or strands of wool in their hair. As they walk along
the village streets barefoot, carrying fruit or flowers in painted
gourds on their heads, they look like exotic queens. For church,
instead of a rebozo, they wear a special huipil, which frames
their faces in lace. They adorn themselves with gorgeous gold
chains, some strung with American ten and twenty-dollar gold
pieces. A group of Tehuanas at church or at a dance is a feast
of color.

Michoacan women, from around Lake Patzcuaro, wear the handwoven wide plaited skirts, of plain black or red wool, held on by several handwoven sashes of different colors, with white cotton, embroidered shirts and the rebozo of the region.

A most extraordinary dress is that of the women of Tuxpan, Jalisco—black wool, plaited skirts, fastened with one narrow, tightly woven sash; white huipil, shaped like a pillow case, with a similar one to cover the head with for church. They are handsome, Aztec types and look especially stunning when coming out of church in groups.

MEN in the marjority wear the unbleached cotton pyjama-style suits. Generally trousers and shirts are of the same material and color but occasionally the shirt is rose-color, pink, yellow or purple. Regional differences are noticeable in the cut of the trousers, the style of the shirts, sarapes, hats.

Otomi men from around Toluca, although poorly dressed in plain white cotton suits, often look very exotic with an embroider-

A Yucatan mestiza.

A totonac woman from Papan-tla, Veracruz

ed *ayate* on their backs, tied in front in the ancient manner. In many villages of the same region, the shirts are quite fancy,

The most dressed up male of.the species is the Huichol, from the Sierras of Nayarit. These Indians wear wide short cotton trousers, loose tunics and around the waist very handsome brown wool handwoven sashes, below which hang strings of small colored wool bags, often several of various sizes, with large bags of different colors hanging from the shoulders. Their hats are low and flat, adorned with gay tropical bird feather or bands of colored wool. Sometimes they also wear beautiful beaded bracelets.

A typical and picturesque man's costume, often very elaborate, is that of the charro, worn by city men and ranchers who ride like the American cowboys. The outfit consists of trousers of leather or striped wool cloth, tightly fitted and adorned with a row of fancy silver buttons on the outside seam of each leg; a soft shirt with flowing tie; a leather jacket, often embroidered or with leather fringe in a yoke form and a large felt sombrero. The city charros use their suits only when they ride, but the ranchers wear theirs all the time, and the regional characteristics are in the differences in cloth, hats, sarapes and so forth, but the cut and style are always the same.

DANCE, PLAY AND CARNIVAL COSTUMES, used by the Indians, are an important and very interesting aspect of the popular arts. The Indians do not use special costumes for their secular folk dances, but they do for all religious dances, plays and carnivals.

In the conventionalized city Jarabe, however, Mexico's national folk dance, the man wears the Charro costume, already described, and the women the China Poblana. The latter consists of a full short red flannel skirt, with a green band at the top, adorned with all-over designs in spangles; a *camisa,* embroidered in fine beads or silk; a folded *rebozo,* on the shoulders and crossed in front; colored ribbons in the hair and red or green slippers. For the stage the dancers often make their skirts of black material and adorn them with silver spangles.

At one time the China Poblana costume, unadorned, was used for daily wear by Puebla women. The legend accounting for its origin relates that centuries ago a pirate ship brought a beautiful and wealthy Chinese princess to Mexico's shores; that the pirates sold her to a rich Puebla merchant; that she embraced the Catholic faith; gave all her wealth to the church and abandoned her costly Chinese dress for this simple one. As she was very much beloved by the women of Puebla, they began to imitate her style of dressing.

There is such a great number and variety in the Indian costumes, that it will not be possible to go into any detail in describing them. Even when used for the same purpose, they differ in

Foto Yañez

China poblanas and a charro from Mexico City

fer in detail in the same groups and in every village. Most of them are made of inexpensive cotton materials, but they are all fantastic and picturesque. An Indian, dressed as a Roman noble, even in a cotton cape, looks the part.

Outstanding among the dance costumes are those of the Apaches or Concheros, a dance which is widespread in the Central Plateau, and the only one in which adult women take part. All the men wear short skirts, pink or some other colored long stockings and *guaraches*; knitted shirts and very fancy headdresses, adorned with beads, feathers and mirrors. The women wear their usual every-day long skirts and waists, but the same type of headdress as the men. Often a group dreses in leather costumes, adorned with fringe of the same material. Those for the Plume Dance of Oaxaca, are of rich brocaded colorful ma-

A plume dancer from Oaxaca

A Carnival costume from Tlaxcala

The Dance of the Moors, Janitzio, Michoacan

terials and consist of snuggly fitted short trousers, stockings, *gua-raches*, shirt of the same material, colored silk handkerchiefs, and a gorgeous headdress, of colored feathers and mirrors. The dancers of the Moors and Christians wear short red trousers, capes and helmets, and there are an infinite number of other costumes.

Costumes for the Holy Week Passion Play represent those which the Indians imagine the Roman judges and soldiers to have worn—capes, suits and helmets with plumes. Neither these nor any of the others used in religious dances, plays and carnivals are historically true, but are very Indian, colorful and fantastic.

For the Fifth of May Battle, near Mexico City, commemorating the victory of the Mexicans over the French, the French and Spanish wear red cotton knee-breeches, coats and soldiers hats. The French have white embroidered cotton cloths, hanging down their backs. In the military-bandit carnival play at Huejotzingo, Puebla, the French and Spanish soldiers' suits are different than those of other villages and some of the groups wear fantastic Mexican and Indian soldiers' costumes, as well as others with long tunics and oriental headdress.

POTTERY

Pottery, together with weaving, are the two most ancient, important and varied of the popular arts. But while there are no pre-Conquest examples of cloth because of its perishable character, we have many of pottery of all the races and epochs. Thus we know that the ancient potters utilized almost all the known technical processes and that they obtained beautiful results.

The tripod bowl with cascabel feet was one of the characteristic forms. Others were vases with globular bodies, supported on three feet; bowls, plates, short-necked bottles, vessels in animal forms and so on. The potters also made many little figures and figurines, the latter with small whistles at the back, which shed light upon the clothing and ornaments of the people. The pottery was ornamented with painted designs in various colors; relief decoration, by means of incision; impression and engraving.

The races that produced the best and most beautiful pottery are those that achieved the highest degree of culture and have already been mentioned—Toltec, Maya, Zapotec, Mixtec, Aztec. Some of the Totonac vases because of their beauty of form, proportion and decoration are considered among the finest of pre-Spanish America.

The Spaniards introduced the wheel, glazing and a more efficient method of firing, through a well-constructed kiln. But even at the present time, as in weaving, the primitive Indian techniques, processes and forms persist along with the European and modern.

Also as in weaving, whole families and villages devote themselves to the making of pottery. There is both a division and interchange of labor between the sexes. Men generally bring the sand, do the firing and carry the heavy loads of the finished product to the market but members of the same family take turns in going. In large centers, however, there are pottery factories, in which the work is specialized.

Pottery-making is a slow process in Mexico, even in large and well equipped potteries, as so much is done in the primitive way, due to low wages—boys or men knead the clay by treading on it all day long; all the decorations are done by hand and so on. The potters who work at home take even longer. They have to bring their sand carrying it on burro-back from long distances and they have no conveniences at all; even their ovens have to be improvised each time, either underground or above with stones, sherds and grass and manure for heating.

It is very difficult to classify and describe all the various regional types of pottery, because there is a great difference in the quality of clays, colors, forms and decorations; but all of it can be divided into two classes—the *corriente* or common, inexpensive, every-day kind, which the poor use, and the expensive kind, made for city people. Although the common pottery is often the chief industry in a village, it is made by isolated potters throughout the Republic. The fine pottery, which is less in demand, is produced chiefly at the present time in the States of Puebla, Oaxaca, Michoacan and Jalisco, but its best period is over long ago. Common pottery, on the other hand, as it is not a product for city stores, conserves its purity and good taste to a greater degree.

Potters, like weavers, have their patron saints in their houses and shops, and they also make offerings to the elements and their pagan gods so that they may have luck in their work.

Pottery-making lends itself to much originality and gives the artist craftsman ample scope to express his talents along various lines, especially if he is working at home.

VALLEY OF MEXICO   OAXACA

The first steps are to bring the sand and to prepare the clay, generally the work of men. Sometimes women make the clay on a metate, in the same manner as the dough for tortillas; men work it with their feet. Four processes are employed in forming the pieces—Modelling, moulding, modelling parts on a piece that has been moulded and modelling with the wheel.

There are three types of finish on the Mexican pottery—the baked, without any gloss, to which I shall refer as "unglazed, the polished and glazed. On the unglazed the painted decorations are applied after the pieces have been dried in the sun and baked; on the other, after it has been slightly baked. Then it is either baked again to fix the colors or polished. The artists use earth colors and brushes made of long dog's hair. The glaze for the better pottery is composed of fine sand, tin and lead and of lead alone for the ordinary.

A primitive kiln, San Anton, near Cuernavaca

COMMON POTTERY is generally glazed, inexpensive and very charming. It is made in all the necessary forms for dishes and cooking utensils for the poor. There are little mugs for children; larger ones for adults; soup bowls; lovely water jars; huge water containers; beautiful large deep bowls for mole, and so on. The colors vary from an orange yellow to a dark ochre, with dec orative touches in yellow and black of simple lines, flowers animals, a verse, a name—a tender thought from the humbl maker to the equally humble user.

In this kind of pottery there are an infinite variety of plain and attractively adroned water and pulque containers; (small figures, animals and other toys, as well as objects made éspecially for holidays,) which will be described later under "Ritual Pottery". In some villages the pottery is very plain and crude and in others a very beautiful unglazed primitive type is made, which never reaches city markets.

THE STATE OF MEXICO produces common pottery only, but of a very good class. Metepec, an attractive agricultural town, a few miles from the Toluca Highway, (market day Mondays), has many potters. They specialize in pulque containers, which because of their shape, are called *canastas* or baskets; large well formed water jars, flower pots. They also make black glazed animal toys, banks and so on. Other villages in the Toluca Valley, where the clay is good also produce pottery, of which the quality is the same. There are, however, differences in color, forms and decorations. In Tecajic the potters make very attractive reddish-brown plates and trays, (charmingly decorated with modelled designs and animals in slight relief.) Valle del Bravo, reached from Toluca and situated in a fertile valley; where the clay is gayly red, produces very attractive pottery, of which some of the jars have forms resembling fruit. (Market day Sundays).

Texcoco potters make a very good, solid, well-finished type of ordinary glazed ware, specializing in the very large *cazuelas* for meats. These are usually plain, adorned around the edges with a different colored band, deriving their beauty from the clay, color and finish. They also make many other objects, among them attractive canastas, with four clay hooks, from which hang cups. In this same region, near the Pyramids of Teotihuacan, a good class of pottery of this same kind is made, together with unattractive unglazed black pieces, which the natives sell to the tourists visiting the pyramids. There is a pottery cooperative in the school of this archaeological zone, where in recent years some very good pieces have been produced, imitating the Puebla. At the present time the potters, under the direction of Concha Michel, in charge of cooperatives, are copying pre-Conquest, regional designs, in modern forms and with modern technique, and securing good results.

Some of the dark brown and black glazed corriente Puebla ware is very beautiful. In it one finds interesting water bottles and large handsome jars, in primitive forms, decorated with mo delled animals and flowers: Sometimes the spouts of coffee and milk pots resemble in form the neck of a rooster, or a pot with two sections for both coffee and milk has a spout for each, a rooster for one and a hen for other. The covers of large water jars are sometimes modelled with a woman's head. As the City of Puebla is noted for its *moles* which require large cazuelas, it is said that those made there are the largest of any in the Republic, some of them measuring over four feet in height and three in diameter. They also make immense water jars, about six feet high and three round. These pieces because of their simplicity, quality and form are very handsome.

Black glazed ritual pottery, which will be described later, as well as toys are also made in Puebla. The potters of Amozoc, Puebla, specialize in clay toys, reproducing beautiful spirited horses, other animals and figures.

PUEBLA pottery is very famous. During the 18th and 19th centuries, when the wealthy classes used pottery dishes and other pieces, it was among the best in the country and together with that made in Tonalá and Tlaquepaque, was exported abroad. Its fame, however, rests on the Talavera, which is the least Mexican.

When the Spaniards established the City of Puebla, in the 16th century, their missionaries who taught crafts as well as the gospel, found excellent potters in the region, once inhabited by the artist Toltec race. So they showed the Indians how to imitate the Spanish Talavera. Contrary to the usual experience this pottery did not take on a Mexican character. Throughout the Colonial Period, the industry was dominated by the Spaniards, who obliged the potters to make faithful copies in form and color of the *Talavera de la Reina* white glazed background with blue designs. As Indian artists are not good at imitating, this pottery was an inferior product. But—, when Mexico won her independence from Spain, through the 1810 Revolution, the Toltec spirit of the potters rebelled also. They began creating a more Mexican Talavera, with added colors and different designs. It was then

A Tlaquepaque jar (original in Popular Arts Museum, Palace of Fine Artes), 36 inches high, modelled by hand; of the polished type; form and design typical of the best Tonala epoch.

Talavera de Puebla

that it became famous, even outside of Mexico, as the *Talavera de Puebla.*

Although the Puebla Talavera took on a more Mexican character in its best epoch, it was and still is a hybrid product, always conserving marked foreign influence in form and manner of decorating—Italian Spanish-Moorish and even Chinese. The best and most beautiful pieces are those made by talented potters, who using the Talavera technique, make Mexican forms and decorate them with Mexican motifs and colors. At the present time Rivero is considered the best decorator of large pieces, which he always signs. They are rare and expensive.

The Puebla Talavera is of good quality; perhaps, the best and least-breakable of any in the Republic, well finished and made into a great variety of forms—vases, flower pots; breakfast and dinner and tea sets; huge jars, some of them showing marked Chinese influence in form and decoration; and very many tiles, adorned with varied designs and pictures. The Churches of Puebla, Cholula and others of the region are noted for their tile domes in all colors, but principally in whites, blues and yellows, the Talavera colors. The decorative motifs are raised flowers, stylized birds, trees and leaves.

OAXACA is one of the most interesting of the popular art states in the Republic, and produces much pottery. The most popular type made in the City of Oaxaca, which is sold outside of the state in large quantites, are the vases, bowls, various other *pieces* complete dinner and tea sets, simply but charmingly decorated with flowers and birds in reds, greens, browns, blues, and burnt orange on a white glazed background. The type from which this is probably an outgrowth still exists and is called *diseño regional.* Only one potter in the city, Ignacio Jiménez, still makes it and is it well-finished and lovely. He uses the wheel instead of moulds; the decorations consist of well defined lines in blue, green, yellow and brown, around the edge of a plate, for example, on a white glazed background, and in the center all alone, in a white space, a beautifully formed hird a duck or heron. Another type of decoration on dishes, which was inspired by the lines of this, is that the all-over designs of zigzaggy-blurry lines, called *modernista* and is very ugly.

An unusual style of pottery, also made in this city, is the white glazed, Mitla ware, decorated with brown greques around the edges, in imitation of the designs on the archaeological ruins of the same name. The potters put it through a lengthy process of four bakings and then carve the design with a stiletto or any sharp point. It is very well made and is said to be the only hand-carved pottery in the world. But the results do not justify the means, for it lacks the Mexican quality of warmth of color and fantasy. There is also a green glazed pottery, made into sets of dishes, vases and so on, named after the other famous archaeological ruins near the city, Monte Alban, because it is decorated without idols in outline, which is even less attractive.

The loveliest of all the Oaxaca pottery, perhaps, is that which comes from the village of Coyotepec. It is made of very good clay unaglazed and unadorned; the color of lead, which is secured in the baking; formed into beautifully shaped jugs and jars of all sizes for water and mexcal. The toys of this same clay and color are especially primitive, humorous and delightful—cows with expressive faces, monkeys playing instruments, tiny birds and animals, all with whistles in the tails and flutes and bells that have lovely sounds. In the village of Santa María Atzompa, across the river from Oaxaca City, the potters make much nice corriente and also a very attractive green glazed ware. The green dishes, platters, vases and so on, are very popular in and outside of the state. Charming toy dishes, frogs and other animals are also made in the green glaze. Much other fine pottery is produced in the State of Oaxaca for regional consumption among which the primitive unglazed jars and other pieces made by the Mijes, of the Sierra of Juárez, is outstanding for beauty of form, color and simplicity of design.

Green Glazed Toys from Atzompa, Oaxaca

Pottery from Tuliman, Guerrero

GUANAJÚATO became a competitor and rival in pottery to Puebla, when the industry was given impulse in that state by the Patriot Priest Hidalgo, in the late 18th and early 19th centuries. The potteries there made beautiful vases, large plates, bowls, dishes and so on, imitating the Talavera quality, but decorating them in the Mexican character, with flowers in greens, sienna, reds and browns, on white and light brown glazed backgrounds. Some of this same type of ware is still being made but it is not comparable to the old. A specialty in the city of Guanajuato, where much pottery is made, are the toy sets of tiny dishes in plain rich glazed browns, greens and blues. Other pottery centers of the state are San Miguel Allende, San Felipe Torres Mochas and Dolores Hidalgo, home of the Cura Hidalgo. All of them make good pottery of the ordinary reddish-brown and some green glazed ware.

AGUAS CALIENTES AND LA PAZ (the latter in the State of San Luis Potosí) are producing some handsome pottery, similar to the Guanajuato semi-majolica type, in quality and decoration, in the form of vases and sets of dishes. They also make the corriente glazed type in those states.

MORELOS produces the corriente pottery only. Much of it from the tiny, picturesque village of San Anton, just across the ravine from Cuernavaca, a popular resort city, is sold to city people. This ware is of a nice tone of red, unglazed, adorned with cream bands or modelled designs, and is made in very primitive fashion. The larger pieces—barrel—shaped pots for plants and small trees, water jars and so on—are the most attractive.

GUERRERO, where so many interesting popular art objects are made, also produces a very beautiful primitve type of unglazed pottery. It comes from the Sierra villages of Tuliman and Guapa, made in the form of plates, bowls, vases and large handsome jars, many of them on three legs, like the ancient ones. The background is of a very pleasing cream-color, achieved by mixing the clay with cotton. The decorations in dark brown are indescribably lovely geometrical designs, stylized flowers, branches, horsemen, figures and so on. Charming primitive animal toys are also made there. Some of this pottery is sold in Taxco,

65

but most of it in Iguala (Market day Sundays). It does not reach city stores because it is breakable and cannot be transported cheaply. The potters have to bring it down from their mountain heights with great care.

Santa Fe, Michoacan

MICHOACAN has beautiful r e d sand and produces, perhaps, more lovely and unspoiled pottery than any other state at the p r e s e n t time. Examples of all of it may be found in the new and very interesting Popular Art Museum, recently organized by Rodolfo Ayala, in Patzcuaro. A simple but pleasing type of pottery is made in Patzcuaro itself. In Tztzuntzan, the nearby ancient seat of Tarascan kings, the potters make lovely sienna, unglazed jars, some with faces, like the pre-Conquest ones; small bowls and other pieces, with cream background and adorned on the inside only, with figures, birds and flowers. Santa Fe, also near Patzcuaro, produces much pottery. The typical type from there is that which is adorned with very gay stylized flowers, on a dark glazed background, in all sorts of interesting shapes. Michoacan kitchens are often hung with strings of tiny pieces of this colorful ware. Not far away from Quiroga, village near Santa Fe, is Nahuatzin, where a very primitive white pottery is made, glazed and adorned on the inside only, with very charming little figures, of the kind a child would draw. Toys are also made of this same ware and decoration.

Santa Fe, Michoacan

In Capula, between Quiroga and Morelia, the potters make graceful highly polished plain dark jars, vases and pitchers, and attractive brown glazed dishes, pleasingly decorated with flowers, leaves and so on. Villa Morelos, near Morelia, reproduces beautiful large bowls, glazed in black on the inside only; handsome jars, the covers decorated with fish and figures as well as lovely toys.

Between Patzcuaro and Guadalajara, along the highway, in Michoacan, are many other pottery-producing villages. Outstanding among them is Huancito, one of the eleven villages of the fertile and picturesque Cañada. From there come lovely polished ochre jars, adorned with primitive stylized designs in black and white, toys and other pieces. Santo Tomas makes glazed pottery and dark pieces, similar to those from Capula.

The most original and beautiful pottery in Michoacan, howver, is that which comes from Patamba, a mountain village, a day's horseback trip distant from Zamora. Here they make jars similar to those of Huancito, with more primitive decorations; lovely green glazed dishes. What they excel in are the large beautiful plates, like the one reproduced here in color. The Contreras family are the best artists of the village. The plates are finished and decorated on both sides, with the principal design inside, of marvelously expressive and fantastic owls, deer and other animals—a bird with wings of leaves; a deer with horns in the form of boughs and equally surrealistic flowers and other forms, in whites and greens, on dark brown glazed background. The Contreras paint these marvelous designs with chicken fea-hers Humberto Arellano once presented them with real paint brushes but they could not use them. Ocumicho, near Patamba specializes in unusual, primitive clay toys, colorfully and charmingly decorated, among which are figures of owls and witches to drive away evil spirits.

JALISCO is one of the States in which some of the very best and most beautiful pottery has been and was still being made up to about ten years ago. As the important pottery villages are very near to Guadalajara, the capital of the state, this ware is always known as *loza de Guadalajara*. It is known, appreciated and sold in every city and market of any importance in the Republic, and during its best epoch was exported to foreign countries.

This popular pottery comes from the villages of Tonalá and San Pedro de Tlaquepaque, a short distance west of Guadalajara. Until about fifteen years ago, Santa Cruz another village near these two, also devoted itself to pottery. In those days the three made distinct types. Since then, however, the potters from Santa Cruz have gone over to Tonalá and Tlaquepaque, and in recent years the Tlaquepaque potteries have taken on potters from Tonalá. As a result, the differences in the styles, although they still exist, are not so defined.

Tonalá used to be more important than the others. Before the Conquest it was the seat of the Tonaltecan kings, and even at that time produced fine pottery. The present day artist craftsmen are the descendents of that race. Now it is a simple village, situated in arid country. The people are dignified and hospitable. The potters invite you into their homes and treat you with beautiful Indian courtesy. They work together in family groups, from grandparents to babies, sitting on petates in the shade of their spacious rooms, corridors or trees.

Formerly the potters of Tonalá modelled all their pieces; painted them with great *cariño*, talent and fantasy, producing the most beautiful clay objects since the Conquest. These were in the form of handsomely shaped covered and uncovered jars, vases, bowls, water-bottles, cups and so on, with unglazed backgrounds either in soft grays or reds, decorated with Indian geometrical and stylized flower, plant and bird designs, in earth colors of gray, grayish-blue, rose, ochre, red and black, all found in the neighborhood. The carbonate of lead for the white was the only imported substance. Another characteristic of this ware was its pleasing scent when it was wet. This was achieved by applying a light coat of varnish of *tierra de Sayula* (another clay from a former pottery village) and fired with *jara* or rock-rose, a process still applied to the unpolished pieces, especially the larger ones, known as *loza de olor*.

Tlaquepaque used to make a limited assortment of glazed pottery, among which the clay toys were outstanding. But during recent years, since the already existing popular demand for the pottery of these two villages has increased so tremendously

Oaxaca mije pottery, light brown background with reddish designs

Tlaquepaque, because it is nearer and more accesible from Guadalajara, has become a more important pottery center than Tonalá. This town is now reduced chiefly to the making of corriente glazed pottery, and even that is no longer as fine as it used to be. All the expensive ware is made in Tlaquepaque. Unfortunately, however, it is not what it was even as recently as ten years ago. Merchants and exporters have so rushed the potters and interfered with their good taste, that only now and then does one come across a fine unglazed piece, decorated in the beautiful old Tonalá manner. Now the large jars are made in moulds, and although the artists still use Indian decorative motifs, they lack the beauty of the older ones. So in Tlaquepaque also the inexpensive pottery remains the best. Specialties here are the famous painted pigs, other very excellent and fantastic animal toys; clay fruit of all kinds and colors; fine religious figures and those of Indians in regional dress, bullfighters and others. There are also good sculptors here, who will model a portrait of you while you wait.

RITUAL POTTERY is always in use, but special objects are made for the three most important religious festivals. As this type of pottery is in the nature of an offering to the gods, some of it is especially beautiful. For Holy Week it is customary to decorate the altars with tender shoots of golden maize and other plants for which new pots are always used. The Atzompa potters make some for Chia, in the form of angels, frogs, pigs and deer, which they adorn partially with a green glaze, leaving rough places for the plant, which is like bristly hair, to take hold. In some Indian churches they reproduce the orchard where Christ was arrested, and put all sorts of animals in the grass.

The Day of the Dead (November 2nd) is another occasion for much new pottery. Special new black glazed candlesticks and incensers are made in many places, very ornately adorned with modelled angels, birds and flowers, like those which are made in the City of Puebla. In the village of Matamoros Izúcar, Puebla, the potters make very handsome and ornate candlesticks and large incensers of baked clay, like the one reproduc-

ed here in color. In Oaxaca one finds primitive, unglazed incensers, on three feet, of brownish color, with cream-colored figures all round the edge, to represent souls. There are also many allusive potterys made at this time — skulls, skeletons and other figures, which amuse the children greatly. In Ocumicho, Michoacan, the boys and girls wage a toy war for this holiday; they put on strings of them and the side that breaks the most wins.

The third festival for which much pottery is made, is the Posadas or Christmas celebrations. Many elaborate mangers are set up in homes and churches, filled with biblical figures, animals, shepherds, regional types of Indians, and so on. They also make tin and clay whistles, which the children blow on in church. The biblical figures are especially interesting because the potters represent them in the robes that they see on saints or in pictures and then give them a Mexican touch by hanging a sombrero down their backs. Often one finds a very charming Adam and Eve under a tree or some other fantastic expression of the Indian's imagination.

HANDMADE GLASS

Glass-blowing is one of the arts which the Spaniards taught the Indians, but they have made it quite their own. The beauty of Mexican glass has achieved fame not only in Mexico, but also in the United States and is carried in the best stores. It is made into complete dinner and tea sets and other objects for household use in rich colors and lovely forms.

Handblown glass is something that even the Mexican poor can afford, for it is less expensive than the ugly imported types. The objects they use, however, are limited to glasses and pitchers, of an attractive greenish color in a ribbed design. Indians may even drink their *pulque* out of these glasses, which, standing in rows on the shelves constitute one of the attractions of a pulquería–a place where they sell pulque, the Mexican drink for the poor.

Glass-blowers are also artists and do not limit their products to utilitarian objects only. They make perfectly formed minute horsemen with riders and other animals and birds, about an inch or two in height. They also make intricate miniature chandeliers and candle-sticks in several colors, and complete sets of dishes in glass closets. In the display rooms of the Avalos Brothers, Mexico City, there is an orchestra of frog musicians, with all sorts of instruments, all of green glass, as well as other interesting fish, animals and figures.

There are large handmade glass factories in Mexico City and Guadalajara, which supply most of the stores. The work is dangerous and poorly paid, but fascinating to watch. The glass is melted in a large oven and the glass blowers take masses of it on the ends of long iron tubes, which they blow into simple or intricate objects before it cools off.

Minature glass horses

GOLD AND SILVER

The ancient Indians made marvelously beautiful things of gold and also some of silver and copper, the only metals they had before the Conquest. They utilized the processes of casting, filagree, hammering in the cold and polishing.

There are many extraordinary pre-Conquest gold objects in Mexican and foreign museums. In the famous collection of jewels and other objects, discovered in Monte Alban, now on exhibition in the Oaxaca City Museum, there are gold, pearl and turquoise necklaces, exquisitely wrought gold pendants, tiger heads, masks and a cup of a natural mixture of silver and copper, a rock crystal goblet and other marvels.

GOLD JEWELRY. Since the Conquest not many Indians have been able to afford gold jewels. The goldsmiths' craft, nevertheless, flourished, for the conquerors had plenty gold. The principal street, in Mexico City, Madero, was for a long time called *La Calle de los Plateros*—The Street of the Jewellers, according to the custom at the time of naming streets after the craftsmen who had their shops on them.

At the present time there are only a few places where Indian women wear gold jewels to a noticeable degree, and they are always made by regional goldsmiths. Oaxaca City is one of them, and since the discovery of the Monte Alban jewels, the goldsmiths there are copying some of the ancient designs in earrings, necklaces and rings. In Tehuantepec. Oaxaca, many of the women display their wealth in gold chains, some twisted like rope and others hung with United States ten and twenty dollar gold pieces and gold earrings. Long filagree gold rosaries with fancy earrings to match are the luxurious adornments of the Indian women of Yucatan. In the State of Guerrero, the goldsmiths of Acapulco and Iguala make some very simple filagree jewelry and necklaces of small gold beads with pendants.

SILVER OBJECTS. During the opulant colonial period in mining, much silver was squandered. Aside from the chalices, candlesticks and so forth, in the churches, altar rails were made of solid silver. There is a legend to the effect that the foundation of the extraordinary church, La Valenciana, of Guanajuato, was laid with silver. The wealthy families had much table ware of heavy silver; as well as candesticks, boxes, goblets, cigarette cases and so on. The silversmiths also being artists, did not limit their production to useful things only, but made many charming little toy figures and objects of silver. Mr. Fred Davis has a collection of over a hundred tiny silver *matracas*, copies of the wooden rattles used during Holy Week, all of different lovely designs. (Drawings of three of them are reproduced here). They are probably from Puebla, where it was customary to make gifts of them at Easter time.

For a long time before and after the 1910 Revolution not much had been done with silver. During the last five years, however, the foreign visitors to Mexico have become interested in silver table ware, and as a result the silversmiths' craft is flourishing anew.

Silver matracas

Silver earrings

SILVER JEWELRY among the Indians is limited to beads, combined with corals, for necklaces and earrings; they do not use bracelets. In villages where there are silver mines, the earrings are especially large and fantastic, some with pendants of animals, flowers and even little pitchers. Those reproduced here are from Fred Davis' collection and they come from the mining villages in the Toluca region.

Silver jewelry has also become popular with tourists and is made and sold in quantities in tourist centers. About ten years ago, when Fred Davis was still in his own Sonora News popular art shop, he began making up some very attractive silver dress jewelry, combining silver with obsidian and jadeite. But since then Taxco has taken the lead in silver jewelry.

The work there was initiated by William Spratling, artist, in his own popular art shops. As there was no tradition in silver jewelry, he is establishing one. He designed beautiful things —broaches, necklaces, bracelets, rings and other objects, with Aztec and Maya motifs, thus creating a style that has a right to exist in Mexico, and he has employed Mexican Indian artist silversmiths to carry out his designs. The Spratling silver is now so well known, that there is a permanent exhibition of it in the Brooklyn Museum and it is on sale in the best United States shops.

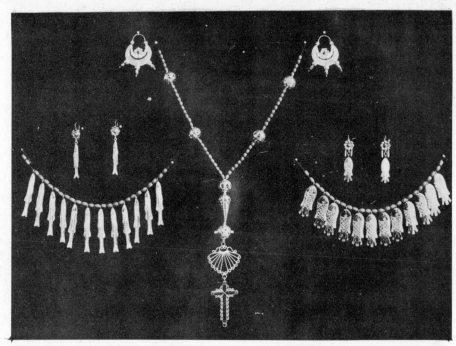

Silver Jewelry from Patzcuaro, Michoacan

Jewels from the collection of Monte Alban, on
exhibitoin in the Museum, at Oaxaca City

IRON - STEEL - COPPER - TIN

IRON was introduced by the Spaniards, who taught the Indians how to work it. Everywhere in Mexico, one sees handsome wrought iron things—fences around churches and houses, window grilling, banisters, huge ornate door nails, knockers, locks, keys and adornments on carved chests. The best iron work, however, dates from the colonial period; comparatively little is being done in iron now.

STEEL is used for spurs and bridle bits and is often combined with silver. Amozoc, Puebla and Leon, Guanajuato are both noted for this kind of work. But the most popular steel object is the *machete*, a long wide curved knife, over a half yard in length. The machete is the Indian's inseparable companion. He uses it for securing and cutting food; to clear away brush in the jungle; for cutting sugar cane and other work, as well as for self-protection. There are very fine machetes, etched with decorative designs and enclosed in handsome leather cases. Nearly all of them have some allusive saying on the blade—"Do not unsheathe me without reason nor replace me without honor." "If this reptile bites you, there is no cure in the drugstore," and others of a less serious nature.

COPPER was known before the Conquest. It is not very expensive and fine large handhammered copper kettles are commonly used by the poor. One of the old pre-Conquest copper centers, where the process has not changed, is Santa Clara del Cobre, near Patzcuaro, Michoacan. The Indians there make lovely pots and dishes of all sizes, which are sold in the Patzcuaro market and stores.

TIN is used very little by the Indians, excepting in lanterns, masks and rattles for dances. And, often they use old tin cans for flower pots. But any Mexican tinsmith can hammer a tin can or a sheet of tin into a work of art. During the last few years it has become very popular with city people and tourists, and is made and sold everywhere. In this line William Spratling of Taxco, has done some original things in candlesticks, picture and mirror frames, flowers and numerous other attractive objects. In tin as in silver Taxco is one of the leading centers.

Courtesy, Manuel Alvarez Bravo

Tin from Taxco

LEATHER WORK

Leather was introduced into Mexico by the Spaniards and is, therefore, a post-conquest art. It is made into *guaraches* or sandals, bags, saddles, belts and coats and is carved, tool, embroidered and apliqued.

Guaraches are very popular with city people and especially with American tourists and are being shipped in carloads to the United States. The large production centers are Oaxaca City, Guadalajara and Mazatlan. The color and weave and shapes are different everywhere—white, browns and the strips are wide or narrow.

Leon, Guanajuato, is noted for its saddles and other leather objects, but they are made everywhere. Belts, pouches and coats are embroidered with gold and silver thread or cord, or designs of contrasting leather are cut out and apliqued on. Saddles are adorned with beautifully formed leather flowers, as well as other objects. Very handsome cases for *machetes* and swords are also a speciality.

The fine dark leather handbags for women, card-cases, bill-folds, and cigarette cases, adorned with geometrical designs, idols and the calendar stones are used by city people only. Weston's popular art store, Mexico City, invented them years ago and they continue one of their specialties.

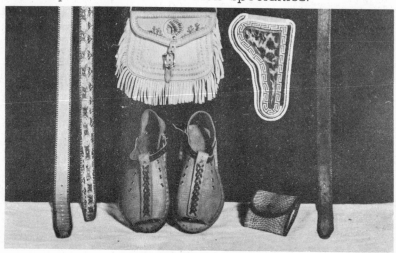

Courtesy, Artes de Mexico

Leather work

CARVING IN STONE - ONYX -
HORN - SHELL - WOOD

Carving is one of the fine pre-Conquest arts, in which the Indians demonstrated great talent, and it is still practiced fairly extensively. In the museums one finds much fine ancient carving in stone and exquisite work on bones. Then there are the stupendous decorations on the pyramids and monoliths.

Since the Conquest an enormuos amount of excellent and very beautiful carving has been done in churches and colonial homes. The choirs of the Mexico City and Puebla cathedrals are excellent examples, and the choir seats of San Agustin, now in the National Preparatory School, also in Mexico City, exquisitely carved with biblical characters and saints. These are but a few examples. Everywhere in Mexico one sees beautiful carving done by the nameless Indian artists.

STONE AND ONYX. Many handsome church altars are carved from fine marbles and onyx. Objects of stone for popular use are the pre-Conquest type of *metates*, upon which the maize is ground and made into dough for *tortillas*; also the *molcajetes* or mortars for grinding. In Veracruz these are made in animal forms like the ancient ones.

There are many states in which onyx is mined, among them Puebla. In the City of Puebla popular artists make many attractive onyx novelties in the form of strings of beads, inkwells, paper-cutters, penholders and others, in light pastel shades. The very bright colors are not natural and sometimes fade.

HORN objects are scarce but here and there one finds a lone vendor selling them on city streets. The horns of young bulls are cleaned and with the aid acids are formed into graceful birds, objects for desks, chessmen and other articles all very lovely.

SHELL is made into a great variety of novelties in Veracruz, Acapulco and other seaports—earrings, necklaces, trays and so on. In Yucatan and other southern states, bordering on the ocean, they make beautiful Spanish combs and earrings of tortoise shell.

WOOD is used for various popular objects. In every market one finds plain orange wood spoons of all sizes and other objects. In Oaxaca the Indians use wooden combs, the handels adorned with charming bird designs. Chocolate beaters are specially attractive. They are turned on lathes, burned and carved with geometric al and bird designs. The same type of adornment is applied to powder, boxes, salt sellers, tooth-pick containers and so forth, for city people. These objects are made around Toluca and in Paracho, Michoacan. In Artes de Mexico, Mexico City, they are having made lovely plain polished wood salad bowls and plates.

Prisoners in all Mexican penitentiaries do very interesting carving in bone and shell. Some of them only discover their talent while there, and with a pointed nail or an ordinary penknife carve exquisite designs on cocoanut shells, make tiny animals of bone, chessmen and other objects, which they are permitted to sell to visitors.

Carved horn   Courtesy, Artes de Mexico

FEATHERS—STRAW—HORSEHAIR

The art of feather work has practically disappeared. Before the Conquest the Indians used to embroider their cloths with colorful feather designs and they wove feather garments. The Tarascans were noted for their beautiful hummingbird feather capes. The only use now made of this kind of work is to adorn Christmas and New Year, place and bridge cards with pretty birds. Colored and dyed feathers are used for headdresses in many religious dances.

Colorful cards and pictures, which show skill and imagination, are made of *popote*, a broom straw. And, of course, there are the many funny looking straw brooms and feather dusters, used in the homes.

Horsehair is dyed and woven into little purses, cigarette cases, and a great variety of small baskets, handles for brushes and, in natural colors, into belts and hat bands. It is a speciality in Morelia, Michoacan and places in the State of Sonora. Prisoners in the Mexican penitentiaries also work with it and sell their products to visitors.

Courtesy Casa Cervantes

Antique carved wood Crucifix

Stone carving in the Merced Convent, Mexico City

Many stores in Mexico City, are displaying large, and for the most part ugly, bateas made there. The lacquer workers who are from Michoacan say they are copies of old designs, but they are decorating them with Charros and China Poblanas, as well as with other false motifs and using linseed oil and analine dyes.

Many stores in Mexico City, are displaying large, and for the
most part ugly, bateas made there. The lacquer workers who are
decorating them with Charros and China Poblanas, as well as

LACQUER

Lacquer is a pre-Conquest art, believed by some investigators to have been introduced by the C h i n e s e, who first came to Mexico about a thousand years before the Conquest. To support this theory there is the coincidence that the important lacquer centers are in the Pacific Coast States of Michoacan and Guerrero, where the Chinese landed; also the similarity in the Chinese and Mexican technical process and stylizations of flowers. Whether this theory be true or not, Mexican lacquer, like all other popular arts, has a definitely Indian-Mexican character.

MICHOACAN lacquer was first made in the villages of Periban, Cucupac and Uruapan. In the first two places the industry has disappeared, but there are some very handsome **Periban** bateas still in existence.

Uruapan, now a very lovely city of about twenty thousand inhabitants, has continued to make lacquer and is the most important center in the State. The two neighborhoods where the Indian lacquer makers live and work are San Pedro and La Magdalena. Recently the government has given them the use of an old chapel in the center of the city, where they make and sell lacquer on a cooperative basis.

Among the many reasons for which an industry or handcraft is carried on in any given region is that of the raw materials it furnishes. In the vicinity of Uruapan one finds the light woods suitable for the bateas or large trays typical of the region and for other pieces. Also the Tarascan Indians discovered that they could extract oil from the Chia seed, of the Salvia Chian, and also from a worm called gie (Cocus Azin), that makes the lacquer hard, unbreakable and waterproof, giving it a quality that no other lacquer has. And the earth of the region furnishes all the necessary colors.

The decorative process typical in Uruapan only is that of incrustation. First the background, generally black is lacquered on the object and permitted to dry. Then the design is cut into the lacquer with a fine steel point and one by one the colors are applied and rubbed in with the palm of the hand, each one being left to dry before another is put on. They also decorated

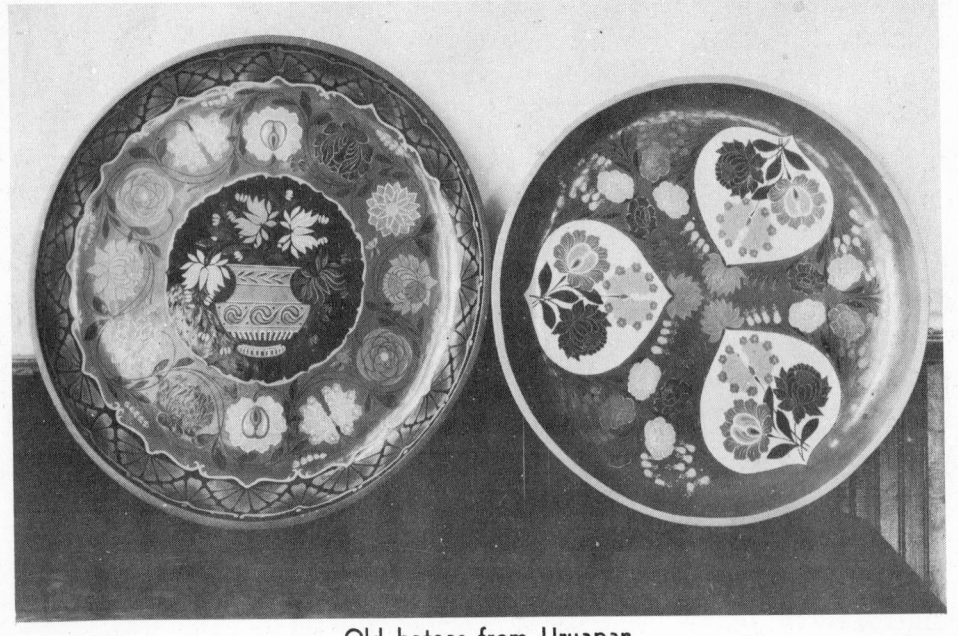

Old bateas from Uruapan

There is, however, a ray of hope for the Michoacan lacquer in what is being done in Patzcuaro. In the Popular Art Museum, recently organized by Rodolfo Ayala, lacquer workers are copying the best of the old bateas and other objects and using pure materials. These may be bought there and at the Cuca Cerda Popular Art Shop. The aim of the Museum is to extend its influence in Uruapan.

OLINALA is the important art center of the State of Guerrero. It is a small picturesque village but difficult to reach, as part of the distance must be made on horseback and it takes several days from the Acapulco Highway. The Indians there are Aztec and very fine artists. The altar in their church, dating from the 16th Century, is uniquely painted by several of the noted lacquer workers with religious subjects in gold or *dorado*, a process for which the village used to be famous.

Guerrero has most of the same raw materials for lacquer as Michoacan, and in addition an aromatic wood, called *olinalau*, of which they make boxes; also the calbash or gourd trees for xicaras and birds and fruit.

their pieces with designs painted with a brush, especially in Quiroga and Patzcuaro, where they sometimes mixed their colors with gold or silver.

Spanish influence on lacquer did not improve the process but enriched the palette with new colors and increased the number of objects that could be lacquered—chests, liters for saints, sewing boxes and so forth, whereas formerly they made only bateas, xicaras (a small gourd bowl) and one or two other items.

Lacquer, like the other important handcrafts, began to decline in the 19th Century, and that which is made in Uruapan at the present time is especially bad. Most of the workers there are substituting linseed oil for aje and chia and prepared dyes for the earth colors and their d e c o r a t i o n s are stilted and ugly. The same is true of the painted bateas of Quiroga. One is no longer sure of the quality of the new ones. And the small boxes, bowls, pin-trays, powder boxes and other objects made to supply modern needs are seldom encrusted.

Olinala lacquer workers, employing the Rayada Process

The process typical of this village is the *rayada* or grooved. First one color is lacquered on and permitted to dry and then another contrasting one, upon which the designs of stylized birds, butterflies and flowers are grooved. Thus the first color is the design and the second one the background. This process was abandoned for a long time. About ten years ago Count René d'Harnoncourt and Mr. Fred Davis discovered some old pieces and got the workers to renew it. They bought all that the workers produced and paid them more for each batea than they are sold for now at retail. The increased demand and the reduction in price is naturally not improving the standard of the work. Yet the production in Olinala is far superior to that of Uruapan.

In Olinala, as well as in the lacquer of Michoacan, the workers also paint decorations. About a hundred years ago they made very beautiful painted chests. The background of these were red or black and they were decorated with flower arabasques and scenes, often copied from foreign postcards, but which the Indian artists transformed so that they became quite Mexican. These chests are still conserved and occasionally one may be found for sale.

An Antique Olinala Chest

Old gourd bowls from Michoacan

Among the very simple, inexpensive, inconspicuous but very charming Olinala lacquer objects are the *jicaras*, which used to be used extensively as ordinary water dippers, fruit and birds, all of natural. The *jicaras* are of half gourds, painted inside and out with charming bird and flower designs, which the water never faded. The fruit are formed into very good imitations of the various tropical and other kinds in the markets and lacquered so that they resemble them almost perfectly. Most delightful of all are the lovely graceful birds. They are glued together of various suitable gourds—a fat one for the body, a slender one for the neck and so forth. The beak is sometimes made of a thorn and the legs of red wood. When the bird is all assembled and shaped, it is glueb to a board, carefully lacquer- One can easily imagine the *cariño* and *gusto* with which theed. artis craftsman makes them. They also make interesantig gourd fish of various sizes.

MASKS

The Mexican Indians, like all other primitive peoples, used masks before the C o n q u e s t . As their civilizations were very advanced, their masks were more varied and of richer materials and better workmanship than those of many other countries.

Our use of masks is for the purpose of disguise, transformation or for the fixing of a facial expression, but for primitive peoples masks are connected with magic and ritual. The Aztecs, for example, before a deer hunt performed a dance in imitation of the chase, which ended with the death of the dancer masked as a deer. They tried to bring about the desired end through the magic of imitation. During their festivals accorded the important dieties, the priests wore masks with the facial characteristics and colors of the gods in whose honor they were given. On occasions masks were placed on idols and effigies of the dead. For the latter the masks were of stone but for human beings they were of wood, mosaics and some of them with hair and golden crests.

Many stone masks have survived the Conquest and may be seen in the museums of Mexico and other countries. In the National Museum, Mexico City, there is a handsome one of diorite, encrusted with turquoise and mother of pearl.

The use of masks among the Indians, continued down to the present time, has greatly decreased with the degeneration of the primitive and religious dances. There are, however, still a great quantity of them being made and worn everywhere.

One of the states producing the finest and greatest variety of masks is Guerrero. A popular dance of this state is the tiger hunt, in which the hunters wear masks in the form of tiger's heads, with spots, hair and tusks. Masks representing other animals, as well as persons, are also made here, and sometimes they are adorned with frogs and serpents.

Michoacan, where there are many religious dances, also has interesting masks. In Uruapan they make very handsome ones in black lacquer. The Yaquis of Sonora make some expressive masks for use during the Holy Week ceremonies and for the Deer Dance. Oaxaca, Puebla and all the other states in which the traditions and dances are conserved, produce masks, which are often crude but always interesting. Saltillo, Coahuila, is noted for tin masks.

Mexican masks are made of wood, cloth, leather, clay, paste, tin and paper, often with genuine hair and teeth. They are painted, lacquered or left in a natural state. The features are subordinated to the materials and one finds in them the same plastic vigor as in the best and most primitive sculptures.

Even the paper masks, which are made in quantities in Celaya, Guanajuato, selling at ten centavos a piece, are works of art, for they demonstrate imagination, fantasy and great decorative talent. Of these special ones are made for the Day of the Dead (November 2nd), in the form of skeletons and skuls. For carnivals they represent French and Spanish types, and at all times, kings, birds, monkeys, as well as all sorts of fanciful faces to the delight of youngsters and adults.

Wooden mask with tin headdress and colored ribbons, worn in the Dance of the Monarch, Village of Naranjo, Michoacan. Courtesy, Popular Art Museum,. Pàtzcuaro

If you were to ask an Indian why he wears a mask in a dance or on other occasions, he would very likely reply, "Es costumbre". Yet the present day Indians are motivated in the use of masks by the same reasons as their ancestors—magic and the desire to achieve an expression for which they feel their own faces inadequate.

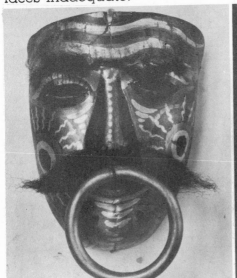

Upper left: Leather apache mask worn in Carnival at Huejotzingo.
Upper right: Wood and clay mask
Below: Wooden masks from the Dance of the Santiagos, Sierra of Puebla

MUSICAL INSTRUMENTS

All popular musicians play on homemade instruments—violins, harps, jaranas (small with strings), guitars, and a larger type called a guitarrón. Although most of them are quite crude in finish, they produce good tones.

Instruments are made everywhere by isolated *maestros*, but there villages in which many devote themselves to the art. One of these is Paracho, Michoacan, where there are many musicians and instrument makers. They make especially well finished and attractive guitars there, which they often adorn with bird designs and encrust with shells.

All musical instruments, with the exception of the harp, are made in toy sizes for children, sold from ten to fifty centavos each, and they can also be played. Indians from the State of Hidalgo, make very tiny instruments, about two inches in length, beautifully finished and inlaid with shell.

Pre-Conquest type of instruments still in use are the tall, round upright drum, *huehuetl* in Aztec, and the *teponaxtli*, a round horizontal one, much in use at the time of the Conquest. Many handsomely carved teponaxtlis are to be found in Mexican museums. They also still use the *chirimías*, reed or clay flutes, some of them in the primitive and others in the modern scale. These instruments are generally played in connection with religious festivals and they produce exotic music.

Conchas or armadillas are the stringed instruments made and played by the Apache dancers, so called because they are of the shell of the armadillo. Often they are attractively painted or inlaid with shells. Indian dancers also use many *sonajas* gourd or tin rattles which they make themselves. Yaqui Indians play on raspadores (wooden rasps) and on half gourds placed over water for their Deer Dance. Indians know many devices for producing rhythm.

VOTIVE OFFERINGS AND CHURCH DECORATIONS

Votive offerings are, perhaps, the most significant expression of the popular arts to the Indians themselves, therefore, the most beautiful. Through them they express their relationship with magical beings; their gratitude for the miracles that make their lives bearable.

Indians love color, so their offerings to their gods are colorful; they love beauty, so their votive offerings are their highest expression of beauty. They still secretly adorn the caves of their hidden idols with flowers, colored ribbons, papers and incensers. Then they atone by giving even more to their saints in the churches. They make beautiful and costly robes for them; embroider altar pieces; give them flowers, candles and incense; entertain them with dances and fireworks on their festival days; and when they help them in their troubles, they bring the pictures of the miracles in paintings and silver to hang in the church.

CANDLE-MAKING is an art, a ceremony and often a pretext for a fiesta, as in the villages of Oaxaca, where they are made by organized groups, called *mayordomias*. Candles are used constantly in churches, homes and huts, so they are made everywhere. There are some of rich orange color wax, of all sizes, often as tall as a person and proportionately thick. Others are of white tallow, with a little fluting of the same substance and adorned with colored tinsel. Wherever candles are sold in stores and stands near churches, they are always hung with artistic care, so that they produce a very pleasing effect. For special occasions large candles are beautifully decorated with flowers, ribbons and tin-foil flags.

In many villages, as in some of the State of Oaxaca and Puebla, Indians make lovely wax decorative pieces in the form of flowers, birds and little animals.

FLOWERS AND SEEDS, especially flowers, are very much used in church decorations. The Indians from Xochimilco and other flower-growing villages, make enormous and very gorgeus floral pieces, which are sometimes combined with seeds, to place around the entrances to churches and special ones for altars. On some occasions they make what they call a tapete

Ritual Pottery and votive offerings. The handsome incenser in the background is from Matamoros, Puebla; the sugar skull, also from Puebla, was made especially for the Day of the Dead. The decoration on the candle is typical of Oaxaca and the black glazed candlestick of many pottery villages.

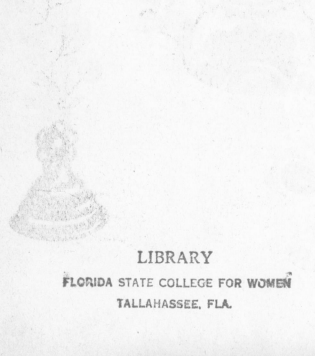

or rug of seeds of various colors, in beautiful designs, or with the image of the saint. Huge funeral floral wreaths are also very popular even among the poor, and the household saint is never without cut flowers. When the Indians cannot grow them, as sometimes happens, they spend their last centavo on flowers in the market place.

CHINA AND PAPIER-MACHE decorations are very popular during festivals, not so much inside as outside of the churches. Various colors of China paper are cut with lovely designs of saints, flowers and other figures and hung on strings crossing the streets. They also use this type of decoration at public dances during festivals and for the inauguration of butcher shops, stores and pulquerías.

Figures are often made for festivals of papier-maché, especially those for the Christmas celebrations, called *piñatas*. They take the form of real and fantastic figures, faces and objects, like aeroplanes and boats, with fringe of China paper. These are used to cover clay jars, filled with sweets, that are broken at every Posada, by some blindfolded person. There is great merriment during the breaking of the piñata and the scramble for the contents.

Luis Marquez

Piñatas

93

RELIGIOUS AMULETS are sold daily at large churches and always at festivals. There are attractive seed rosaries, sometimes combined with bright-colored wool or ribbons, with a silver cross or madellion; silk madellions on ribbons or cords; pictures of the saints on pins; sacred hearts; very attractively painted wooden frames for saints pictures and so on. It is customary for persons who attend festivals or pilgrimages to purchase them, have them blessed for themselves and to take home as gifts.

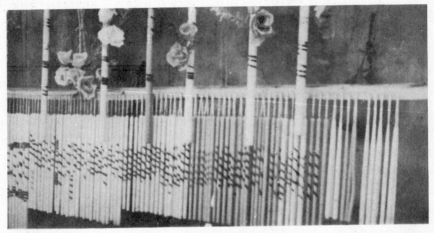

Candles for sale at Chalma Sanctuary

RETABLOS are painted miracles. A man is falling down the shaft of a mine; he prays to his patron saint and is saved. Someone is ill, dying, there is no hope. The family weep and pray to their household saint; the patient recovers. The persons to whom such miracles happen, go to a popular artist, who devotes himself to this kind of work, tells him the story and he paints it either on tin, copper or canvas. Then it is hung in the church near the saint, who has interceded. There are innumerable retablos in churches, where the saints are especially miraculous, many of them very beautiful pictures. They are genuine Mexican popular paintings—realistic pictures of super-realistic events; painted with great sobriety and sensitivety and profound recognition of a truth that makes a miracle of reality and reality a miracle.

94

SILVER MILAGROS or miracles, are the reproductions in silver of parts of the body, persons and animals, that have been cured or helped in some way through a miracle, to be hung in the church as an expression of gratitude. There are many beautiful old milagros, because formerly they were made by hand, beautifully formed of heavy silver, but those that are used now by the poor are made in moulds and are very light weight.

Old crucifix, figure of maise paste, croos of gilded plaster and mirrows.

FIREWORKS

Gun powder was an important factor in the Spanish Conquest of the Mexican Indians. It was new to them and so were fireworks, but the latter appealed so to their imagination that they have imcorporated them into their religious ritual. At important festivals the patron saint is greeted at dawn with song and salvos and at all festivals masses are announced with daylight fireworks. The poorest villages will collect and save all year long about two hundred pesos for a castle for the big festival, a fortune for the Indians, to be burned up in twenty minutes of dazzling beauty.

Every village or district has firework-makers, who are genuine artists. The work is poorly paid and dangerous, but they love it. Between festivals they work in the fields or at other occupations. In large centers there are fireworks shops in which the work is fairly constant. Oaxaca City is one of them and the workers there are noted for their skill and ingenuity. They not only make all the usual pieces but very excellent stylized portraits of historical personages, which are burned on the main plaza on the eve of the 16th of September, Mexico's Independence Day.

The most beautiful and intricate of all the fireworks pieces are the castles. In these the artist's fancy may run riot. They reproduce saints, crowns, crosses, flowers and birds. Often they are a hundred feet tall, and each piece is so placed that it goes off separately. Sometimes they last as long as twenty minutes and then go out in a shower of beautiful luminous light. There are also daylight castles, with humorous figures of animals and dolls, that embrace and dance as the fireworks go off.

Notable among the fireworks pieces are the little bulls, which a man wears over his head and plays at bullfighting while the fireworks are being shot off. It is a dangerous feat, but great fun for the crowds.

Another popular type are the figures of Judases. They are of papier-maché, varying from one to ten feet in height, with funny expressive faces, which are burned on the streets after the Mass of Glory, on Saturday of Holy Week. Store-keepers use them for advertising purposes. They stretch a rope across the street and tie a Judas to it. If the storekeeper is a baker, he hangs strings of bread on his Judas; if a butcher, sausages and so forth. The Judas dangles on the rope until the crowd gathers after mass. Then the fireworks are set off and he goes to pieces amidst noise and smoke, and the boys make a grand rush for the spoils.

There is no limit to the variety of objects the fireworks makers invent. Among the festivities for the inauguration of President Lazaro Cardenas, 1934, was a Mexican Night, on the Lake, in Chapultepec Park. The fireworks for the occasion were stupendous and among them was a miniature naval battle. The pieces were made by the workers from the State of Chiapas and were indescribably beautiful.

A Judas in the Home of Diego Rivera.   Lola Alvarez Bravo

TOYS

The Mexican toy world is delightful, imaginative, fantastic, a proper one for the escape of children whose lives are filled with the hard realities of life. From the time they are mere babies they dress like their parents and share in their hard labors. But there is this paradox, that although the children begin being adults when they are still practically infants, the adults never outgrow their childish delight in simple, amusing and beautiful things. Thus the craftsmen who make the toys are happy in their work and they put into it much affection, joy and humor. They also love toys.

If all the toys that I have described under other headings petate, pottery, glass and so on, were all together, they would constitute a great ensemble of grotesqueness, beauty and humor. There would be little clay insects, birds and animals of all sizes, forms and colors, with whistles in their tails; animals playing instruments; pigs painted in colored coats, adorned with gay flowers; petate and tin rattles and many more amusing things.

Many of the clay animals are intended for banks, so have slits on their backs, but often the toymakers forget to make them big enough for a centavito to pass through. The children, however, never discover this defect, for they have no centavitos to save. But what they are always aware of and take delight in are the forms and colors, and the comical expressions.

In addition to the ordinary every day toys, there are a great variety of charming seasonal ones, which afford much fun for children. For Holy Week, for example, there are the wooden *matracas* to make noise with; for the Day of the Dead (November 2nd), candy skulls, little cardboard coffins from which jump skeletons when a string is pulled, skeleton masks and similar objects; for the Posadas, the Christmas celebrations, *piñatas*, all the biblical figures, shepherds and animals, beautifully formed in clay.

There are also many lovely housekeeping toys—furniture of all kinds, tiny sets of dishes, perfectly formed, finished and glazed; stone *metates* and *molcajetes* for grinding, little *braseros*

Clay toys from various parts of the country. (The second
figure from the left, on the middle shelf, is of petate). The toy to
the left on the lower shelf is a merry-go-round. The shelves upon
which the toys are displayed, called *trasteros*, carved in the Michoacan manner, are especially fine; but ordinary ones are used
everywhere and may be purchased in city markets.

or stoves; in fact, everything that is used in a house is reproduced in miniature for children. Dolls are generally made of cloth and dressed like the adults of the region. Recently some dolls are being made with porcelain heads and dressed in China Poblana and Charro costumes and others of better materials to sell in city stores.

Not all the Indian children can afford the toys described above, but all of them can afford some, especially those made by potters and other craftsmen in their own regions. When they cannot buy all the toys they want, they are very clever and ingenius at inventing them. Instead of a stone metate for making their *tortillas*, they use a board or ordinary stone; they make dolls of rags and so on. Their make-believe world is always an adult world. But the Indian adult world has much that is make-believe in it--the belief in magic and miracles.

Clay toys from Tlaquepaque

A reconstructed kitchen in the Popular Arts Museum at Patzcuaro

Showing a woman making tortillas, the metate on which the maize is ground and the comal on which they are baked

KITCHENS do not exist in Indian huts, but in real homes they are often the most attractive room in the house. The furnishings consist of a *brasero*, a stove of Spanish origin, generally of plain red but sometimes of fancy tiles, with holes on top for the charcoal, upon which the pots are placed and others at the side for fanning the coal into a flame; a table, chairs and on the walls numerous pottery pots and dishes, of various sizes, hung in harmonious compositions. In large homes and haciendas the kitchens are very large with high ceilings, and they are always alive with many cooks and their assistants, for Mexican dishes require much help.

POPULAR DISHES. Those of us who believe with Feuerbach that "Der Mensch ist was er isst," or "Man is what he eats," will, naturally, expect Mexican food to be rich, plastic and colorful, and will not be disappointed. Mexican dishes appeal not only to the palate but also to the eye.

The most festive and luxurious of the Mexican dishes is mole de guajolote (mah-leh, a rich, heavy spicy sauce; gwah-hoh-loh-teh. Aztec for turkey). Mole is made of a variety of chiles, with almonds, spices, sesame seed and sometimes chocolate. Before the Conquest it was made with less ingredients and was called *chilmolli*. It is a costly dish, but at sometime or another all Indians can afford it, and the pieces of turkey, covered with rich brown mole in the huge pottery bowls, is very lovely.

The Indians' bread is the tortilla, made as before the Conquest—a thin pancake, of corn previously soaked in lime, ground on a metate and baked on an iron griddle. Many things are made of tortillas—when spread with chopped meat, chicken or cheese and rolled up, they become *tacos* or the Mexican sandwich; when the tortillas are fried and filled with chicken or cheese and covered with mole or some other spicy sauce, they are *enchiladas.* A tortilla filled with cheese, potatoes or meat, doubled like a turnover and then fried in lard, is a *quesadilla*. Tortillas fried crisp and spread with chopped meats or salad are *tostadas*. All of these tortilla combinations and the other Mexican beans, rice, egg and meat dishes are delicacies and lux-

Bread for the day of the dead

uries for most Indians; their principal diet consists of plain tortillas black beans cooked in water, chile and sometimes boiled coffee.

SWEETS (dulces in Spanish, including candies) are made of fruit, milk, sugar, seeds, in bright colors and attractive forms, sometimes of birds and animals. Even sweet bread is made into figures and animals. One of the chief attactions at festivals are the little tables of gay candies and cakes of all kinds. For the Day of The Dead, they make sugar skulls and animals, with designs of colored beads and tin-foil.

DRINKS. The national alcoholic drink which the poorest can afford, is *pulque*, made of a juice sucked from the heart of the maguey, called *aguamiel* or honey water, which when permitted to ferment, becomes intoxicating. Other national and inexpensive alcoholic drinks are tequila and mexcal, made, of special squat maguey plants. *Aguas frescas* or sweet drinks are always made of fruit and seeds, which take on their natural colors —orange, pineapple, strawberries and so on. These drinks are sold everywhere, on street corners in cities, at market places and festivals.

HOUSES—FURNITURE—POPULAR PAINTING

HOUSES of the people have not changed much since the Conquest. None, naturally, have survived, but the descriptions in the early chronicles and pictures in the codices give one an idea of how they were. Most of them on the Central Plateau and other parts of the Republic are of adobe—sundried mud bricks, with tile roofs. Those of the hot regions have walls of bamboo sticks or twisted reeds, with roofs of palm leaves, tree bark or grass. Some of the adobe houses are covered with a mixture of lime and sand and painted white or in lightcolors. None of them have floors. In shape they are either square or oblong, often several huts form a compound.

Indian huts are very picturesque, especially those of light brown adobe, with red tile roofs, nestling against a green hillside. The villages themselves are often charming, with their lovely gardens and cactus or stone fences. But the construction is not hygienic, since the materials themselves are carriers of dust and insects. The Federal Health Department is now making a study of those conditions, with a view to improving them.

Typical mestiza houses of Yucatan

Equipales, a painted chair with fibre seat and Toluca sarape.

FURNITURE is very simple. In most huts there is none —petates serve as beds and there may be a few tiny wooden-stools to sit on. Some of the Indians, however, are now using tables and chairs. The chairs are homemade with reed bottoms and the wooden legs and backs painted either in plain colors or adorned with flowers. Almoloya del Rio and Tenancingo, in the Toluca region, are the two leading villages where such chairs and stools are made. Indians in and around Guadalajara, Jalisco, make *equipales,* seats and backs of cowhide, in shape like those used before the Conquest, which are sold in Mexico and other city stores. Those painted with Indian heads are a speciality for city people. Around Tepic, Nayarit, the equipales are of wood and reed or palm, probably exactly the same materials as were used by the ancient Indians, since at that time they had no cowhide. When the Indians do not sleep on the ground, their beds consist of sticks on a rough wooden frame in the tropics or of boards on four crude legs, with the petate serving as mattress.

Adobe and reed huts

DECORATIVE PAINTING in connection with Indian huts or houses is limited to the adornment of chairs or the painting of walls and doors, but often the popular artists are employed to decorate places frequented by the poor—fondas or hole-in-the-wall eating joints, butcher shops and pulquerias. The first is generally painted with peaceful scenes; the theme of the decorations on butcher shops is that of the butcher being chopped up and cooked by the animals, everything reversed. The best and most interesting mural decorations are on the pulquerias. For a time during the Diaz dictatorship they were forbidden, but since 1910 they are again in evidence.

The pulqueria decorations are among the most excellent of the Mexican art expressions. They are original, express their environment and the character of the people perfectly and plastically fulfill all the conditions of works of art. One sees in them the Mexican love of bright colors, the irony and mocking humor, always bordering on the tragic, the laugh with the tongue in the cheek—that untranslatable because it is so essentialy Mexican—*vacilada*.

A very essential part of the pulquería decorations are their names, which if not invented by the artist are painted by him with the same mastery and expressiveness as the forms and figures, which they describe. Here are some of them—"The Lady of the Night" (a tragic looking lady in white, in the background a full moon reflected in a body of water; on the facade of a pulquería in a questionable neighborhood). "My office." "My Illusions." "At Night We Shall Meet." "The Kissable Lass." "Wise Men Without Studies." "Recollections of the Future." "The Dry State." "Los Changos Vaciladores"—a delightful painting of monkeys having a gay time.

All sorts of other shops—groceries, bakeries, drugstores and so on, have poetic and expressive names. A store in Cuernavaca, where coffins are sold is called "Quo Vadis."

Other very important aspects of popular painting are the *retablos*, described under Votive Offerings, and portraits. There are some excellent portraits of the 18th and 19th centuries in private homes and museums, especially in the one at Guadalajara. These also show the same ability to adapt the subject matter to pictorial expression as is found in other popular painting. Besides portraits there are the numerous beautiful religious paintings in churches and convents, which are more proof of the great plastic ability of these nameless artists. The subject is a vast one and deserves a whole book, with many illustrations.

A Decoration on a Pulqueria in the Federal District.